PRAISE FOR
THE SECRET BLEND

"*The Secret Blend* is one of the best books on relationships I have ever read. I will never look at coffee or friendship the same! What a brilliant concept!"

—Debra White Smith,
best-selling author of the Seven Sisters series

"Buy ten copies of Stan Toler's book and give nine away. Then get together with those nine people over a cup of coffee and share how *The Secret Blend* has changed your life."

—Dr. Neil T. Anderson,
author of *Victory over the Darkness*

"In a world moving at the speed of light, we need to be reminded of simple lessons that make each day rewarding. The seven lessons of *The Secret Blend* will help you enrich your life beyond your wildest expectations."

—Leslie Yerkes,
founder and president of Catalyst Consulting Group and coauthor of
Beans: Four Principles for Running a Business in Good Times or Bad

"In *The Secret Blend*, Stan Toler helps us focus on what matters most: our relationships with the people in our lives. As we share in the truths that Joe learns at Mac's coffee shop, we experience a deeper awareness of our own thirst for true friendships and how to obtain them. I can't wait to share this book with my friends!"

—Andy Andrews,
author of the *New York Times* bestseller *The Traveler's Gift*

"*The Secret Blend* is a get-rich book that will increase your net worth in all the right places. My good friend, Stan Toler, is a man who knows the ups and downs of life. So if you'd like more joy and fulfillment in your life, then *The Secret Blend* is just the cup of refreshment you're looking for. It's good to the last page!"

—Martha Bolton,
former staff writer for Bob Hope and author of more than fifty books,
including *Didn't My Skin Used to Fit?*

"A college professor once told me, 'Everybody has at least one book in them.' Stan Toler has a lot of books in him, and *The Secret Blend* is probably his greatest, his signature book. Stan realizes that *relationship* is the strength of ministry and the power of a personal Christian walk. If you want to get close to Stan's heart, learn the secret of his success, and discover how you can build your life on relationship, this is a must-read."

—Elmer L. Towns,
vice president of Liberty University and dean of the School of Religion,
Liberty University, Lynchburg, Virginia

THE
SECRET
BLEND

A PARABLE
OF RICH
RELATIONSHIPS

STAN TOLER

WITH FOREWORD BY JOHN C. MAXWELL

BEACON HILL PRESS
OF KANSAS CITY

To Linda, my best friend and wife of forty-one years.
Love, Stan

FOREWORD

The Secret Blend is a great book. Having said that, I do have to confess that it's very hard for me to write an unbiased foreword for Stan Toler's new book. And really, would he have honored me with the privilege of writing this if I wasn't going to say it's great?

First of all, Stan and I go way back. We were boyhood friends. My dad, Dr. Melvin Maxwell, was his college president and encouraged him to follow his call to the ministry. Anyone mentored under my dad's ministry was one of his boys for life; that makes Stan and me brothers.

Stan and I attended college together. When I started out in the ministry as pastor of a church in Ohio, the first staff member I ever hired was Stan. That began a fruitful professional association. Through the years we have had countless opportunities to work together and maintain the closest of friendships. So you can forgive me for gushing about this book. Stan truly is one of my closest friends. But there's another reason I'm highly biased about how great this book is. Stan may not agree with me, but I'm claiming credit for the whole thing—well, at least it was half my idea.

Stan and I were sitting in a restaurant with our mutual friend, Dr. Elmer Towns, talking about what makes each of us unique in our approach to life, the hallmark of our service in this world. We were encouraging one another to keep growing and to keep doing what we were best at. Not surprisingly, Stan urged me to keep my focus on leadership development. He implored Elmer to stay the course with his writing on spiritual disciplines.

When it was Stan's turn to sit under the microscope, Elmer and I said at almost the same instant, "Stan, you need to write a book about relationships." We both knew that no one cares more about people than Stan does. People instinctively and instantly know it— and they love Stan in return. He probably has more good relationships than any other person I know! He's simply the best.

So when Stan puts on paper an absolutely entertaining story to teach us how to become truly rich, you need to understand that he knows what he writes about—and now I'm being perfectly objective. If the quality of our relationships is the most accurate measure of our wealth, Stan Toler truly is a fabulously rich man.

If you follow the simple but profound wisdom of this book, you, too, will become wealthy beyond anything you've ever experienced.

Enjoy!

—John C. Maxwell,
founder of The John Maxwell Company and
author of *The 21 Irrefutable Laws of Leadership*

ACKNOWLEDGMENTS

Special thanks to Jeff Dunn for creative insight and editorial assistance. Much gratitude to Jerry Brecheisen, Debra White Smith, and Jim Wilcox for editorial support and ongoing friendship. God bless you all!

CHAPTER 1

RAIN pelted the sidewalks of Seattle. Not your gentle, springtime, garden-variety rain. This was a downpour, a *drencher*, an old-fashioned *gully washer*. This was a rain that seemed to say out loud, "I'm miserable, so you may as well be too." It had started early that morning and didn't seem to have any plans to let up. The steady runoff was too much for the street drains to handle, so the water pooled on the asphalt, giving way only when a car invaded its borders.

One car on the road that morning was no stranger to dismal weather. This car had seen it all: light rain, heavy rain, snow, blizzards, hail, sleet, ice. The only weather condition the car seemed to have avoided was two sunny days in a row. The driver was also used to days without sunshine, having lived all his life here in the Northwest, but that didn't mean he was accustomed to the rain.

He felt the dampness inside his car. Perhaps it was because his car was ten years old and the driver's side window had an arthritic condition that kept it from climbing all the way to the top of the window casing. The rain spotted the weakness and exploited it fully. But somehow this morning it felt as if the rain were coming up from the ground, through the flooring of the old car, into his very bones.

Thus was Tuesday in the life of Joe Conrad.

It could be worse, he thought—and soon it would be if he didn't get something warm into his body. Although his morning beverage of choice was a diet cola, the dismal damp of this morning spoke to his very being and demanded a cup of hot coffee. "Yes!" he responded to the demand. So Joe Conrad turned right onto Ventura Street, remembering that gas station only a block out of his way where they would surely grant him a cup of steaming black coffee.

And they would have been glad to, had it not been for the robbery that had taken place earlier in the morning.

Joe pulled into the station's parking lot only to be met by a police officer in a yellow rain slicker. Yards of yellow tape were strung around—from the fence post by the station all the way to the old-fashioned, serve-yourself gas pumps. "DO NOT CROSS." The officer slowly made his way to Joe's car, one hand in the parka's side pocket, the other holding a cup of coffee—which immediately caught Joe's attention.

"What's going on?" Joe shouted through the window opening.

"This store is closed for now, sir," the policeman answered. Then, after a casual sip from the coffee cup, the policeman added quite formally, "We're investigating a crime. You'll have to move along."

"I just want a cup of coffee," Joe pleaded. "I'll only take a second."

"Sorry," the officer replied firmly. "We've got police work to do here."

Joe obediently drove back onto Ventura. *Well, coffee would have been great, but maybe I'll just settle for a cola.*

Then he remembered his neighbor talking about a new coffee shop. *Where was it?* He vaguely recalled something about it being near the dry cleaners, farther down Ventura. *I'm this far out of my way. One or two more blocks won't hurt.*

When he got to the strip mall where the dry cleaners was located, Joe was momentarily taken aback. There was the coffee shop. A sign in big, bold, neon letters read, "Mac's Place." Underneath, in smaller letters, it said, "Coffee, Tea, and Kindness." He thought, *But where is the dry cleaners?* Then it dawned on him: The coffee shop was where the cleaners had been. *They didn't last long,* Joe observed. *But then again, what business does anymore?*

He parked and waited a couple of minutes before getting out of his car. He hoped the rain would settle down at least to a steady downpour before he made a dash to the glass door at the front of the shop. While he waited, he rehearsed the day ahead. One more get-together with his team to make sure all bases were covered, then a midmorning meeting with his new, and potentially best, client. If their marketing committee liked what they saw this morning—and signed off on the deal, making it official—Joe would be a wealthy man by this afternoon—at least wealthy by his standards. Joe's share of the nearly ten-million-dollar advertising campaign he was proposing would come to more than a hundred grand, plus a nice bonus that his boss had all but promised him. He needed this contract. He needed the money. But right now what he really needed was a good cup of coffee to raise his falling body temperature and his sagging spirits.

The deluge didn't let up, so Joe made a dash for the door anyway. It was only twenty feet or so to the coffee shop's entrance. But the shortness of the distance was no match for the magnitude of the rainwater. Joe got soaked—through his sports coat to his freshly ironed dress shirt. *Great! Just great!* he thought. His entrance couldn't help but attract the attention of those already sitting at the half-dozen or so tables scattered around the shop. A real wood fire was burning in a large stone fireplace, and two women sat in chairs in front of the fire, each with an oversized coffee mug in her hand. A man and woman sat at one of the tables—*husband and wife, perhaps,* Joe guessed. Heads nearly touching, they were talking quietly over their hot drinks. A father and daughter shared another table, looking concerned about some schoolwork that was most likely due later that morning. At yet another table sat three men: one in a suit, the other two in jeans and sweatshirts, each with a similar-looking black book in front of him.

"Would you like a towel?" asked a friendly voice from behind the counter.

"Excuse me?" Joe responded to the voice, noticing for the first time the beautiful carved-wood bar in front of him. Stacked in front of it were light brown burlap sacks, opened at the throat and overflowing with darker brown coffee beans. Shiny chrome pots lined the counter. Small cards hung from small, simulated-gold chains over each spout. Each card had a name: Mac's Blend, Kenya Peaberry, and Assam Golden Tip Tea. Beside each pot were two stacks of cups; on the left were dark green ceramic mugs, and on the right were beige paper cups with the store's logo imprinted on them.

"You look like you might need a towel to dry off," repeated the man behind the counter. "That's a hard rain a-falling," he said with a chuckle, enjoying his little takeoff on a Bob Dylan song.

Joe looked at the character behind the bar, wondering what kind of person would be quoting Dylan to new customers. The man appeared to be in his fifties—Joe was thirty-two—and was tall and lanky, but not too thin. He wore khaki shorts and a T-shirt that bore a large logo of Mac's Place, along with a few stains. His hair was a mop of red, and its owner seemingly allowed it to wander freely, like a two-year-old grandson in a toy store.

"Er, yes, that would be great," Joe finally said. The man handed him a thick bar towel, neatly folded. Joe quickly unfolded it and dabbed at the water on his face, then his hands, and then his hair. "Thanks. I probably need a complete change of clothes," the wet-like-a-mop customer tried to explain.

"Can't help you there," said the coffee man. "We don't do extra clothes in this shop. Besides, you'll get just as wet when you go back outside. I'd be happy to loan you an umbrella. You can bring it back next time you come in."

"Well, I'm not a regular customer. I don't even drink coffee that often," Joe struggled. "For some reason, I just had a craving for coffee this morning."

"Sure. By the way, the name's Mac." He extended a hand toward Joe.

"I'm Joe," he said as they clasped hands firmly.

"Welcome to Mac's Place, Joe. Would you like a cup of our Mac's Blend?"

"Uh, sure," Joe answered hesitantly. "Is that just regular coffee?"

"There really is no such thing as regular coffee," Mac replied in a friendly way. "All coffees are unique, just like people. Even the same variety of coffee bean can be different from tree to tree. Like coffee, we all have our own experiences that make us into who we are. But that's what makes this world great, isn't it?"

Joe looked at Mac, ready to answer his question. There wasn't time. Mac was speaking again.

"I think you'll like the flavor of Mac's Blend—it's our house blend. It has a slight hint of . . . well . . . I don't want to spoil it for you. I'll let you tell me."

"I'm in kind of a hurry this morning," Joe replied even though he didn't have to be at the office for another forty-five minutes or so. He just didn't feel like talking about coffee—or people, for that matter. Besides, coffee was coffee, wasn't it? *Who does he think I am? One of those Seattle coffee connoisseurs? I just need a little warmth on the inside. But I'll have to admit that a little coffee conversation might be a small price to pay for some hang time near that fireplace.*

"Then you'll want this to go," Mac said as he filled a large paper cup from one of the pots and fixed a plastic lid on it. "There you are."

"How much?" asked Joe, reaching for his wallet.

"No charge to our first-timers," said Mac with one of those I-know-something-you-don't looks.

"Really, I don't mind paying," Joe responded.

"We rely on repeat business," Mac smiled again. "We think that if you like how that first cup tastes, you'll come back often. Take it with my compliments. And here's a coupon for you to use the next time you come by."

"Oh," he added, "be sure to hang on to that towel. You'll probably need it when you get to work, too."

Joe thanked Mac once again as he took the hot cup of coffee and a brightly colored piece of paper—which he stuffed into his pants pocket—and braced himself for the run to his car.

And, just as Mac had suggested, he was glad for the towel once he got to his office building. The rain was coming down even harder. He reached his desk with the hot coffee in his left hand, while he dried himself with the towel in his right hand. He hung his thoroughly soaked sports coat on his chair, hoping against hope it would dry before his highly important meeting. As he transferred his car keys from his coat pocket to his pants pocket, he felt a piece of paper. *Am I supposed to call someone? Am I supposed to get milk from the store on the way home?* When he pulled out the damp, bright yellow piece of paper, he realized it was the coupon from the coffee shop.

"One free cup coffee or tea" read one side of the paper.

Joe turned it over to see if there was something on the back. There was. And what was written on the back of that yellow slip of paper would change Joe's life forever.

CHAPTER 2

"NEXT, we want to show you the storyboards for the initial TV campaign." Amanda Wright was the media director assigned to Joe's creative team. She was twenty-five, perky, if not outright cute, and polished beyond her years as a presenter. Joe thought she was married or at least had a steady boyfriend. Though they had worked side by side for the past two years, he knew very little about her, except that she was an excellent media director.

Amanda adjusted the easel that stood at the front of the conference table and held six poster boards. Each had a scene from a sixty-second television commercial sketched on it with colored markers. Amanda described the action as D'Juan Dixon and Leslie Phelps, two creative assistants, read the male and female role lines from the script. Amanda changed the boards to keep up with the story line. In this way, the marketing team from AguCo Foods could "see" the commercial that Joe's team was proposing for its new line of Tex-Mex restaurants.

AguCo was one of the largest food conglomerates in the nation. Its holdings included soft-drink bottlers and distributors, packaged-food companies, full-service and fast-food restaurants, and an industrial food division. AguCo was also nationally acclaimed for supplying prepared meals to schools, hospitals, and corporate cafeterias. It was looking for a "cutting edge" ad agency to promote its new La Papa Caliente (The Hot Potato) fast-food chain. Joe's agency, Stuart Creative Media, had never made a presentation to a client as big as AguCo. It had some regional campaign successes under its belt, but nothing of this magnitude. The agency had never managed a campaign with a budget of more than three million dollars. If it landed the AguCo contract, there would be a three-year deal, with the first year's budget set at one million dollars and promised increases in years two and three. This would make Stuart Creative Media a "player" in the Northwest, allowing it to attract other major companies.

Joe and his team—Amanda, D'Juan, Leslie, Mark Johns (media planner), and Maria Alicia Hernandez (administrative assistant)—had prepared nearly six weeks for this meeting. The marketing team from AguCo would not make the final decision. Technically, they had to make a recommendation to the AguCo board of directors, but in reality, that was a rubber stamp. This presentation could determine if Stuart Creative was edgy enough to reach the target audience AguCo wanted for its La Papa Caliente stores: Sixteen- to twenty-four-year-olds who could be persuaded to try "Fresh-Mex" tacos and burritos, as well as potatoes fully loaded and crowned with Mexican spices and sauces.

The conference room had an impressive blond oak table, twelve chairs (each in a different style, just to give an impression of eclecticism), a white board on one wall, and a credenza with snacks and drinks (all AguCo brands, of course) against another wall. A third wall of sparkling clean glass revealed a sigh-inspiring view of the Seattle skyline. Everyone (except Amanda, who was standing at the easel) was seated around the large table. Most had selected flavored bottles of water, but Leslie and Maria Alicia were drinking hot herbal teas. Joe was still working on the last tepid ounces of coffee from Mac's Place.

The coupon was still in Joe's pocket. He had stared at it for several minutes when he first arrived at his office that morning and had reread the back at least five times since. He acted as if he just couldn't believe what was written on the back of the coupon! Even now, in the middle of the most important presentation of his career (of his life!), he couldn't shake the words on that slip of paper out of his mind.

At first Joe thought it might be some marketing ploy for a new coffee drink, probably loaded with rich cream and seductive flavors. *Weren't those fancy coffee places always coming up with strange new drink combinations? For people like those two aristocratic brothers on TV who always ordered lattes and cappuccinos at their snobby little coffee hangout. This was probably just Mac's way of getting customers to buy a new "richer-tasting" coffee.*

But that couldn't be it—I didn't notice any of those large, silver machines that foamed milk and all that. Then he thought, *It's probably a multilevel marketing scheme of some sort. Of course! "Do you want to earn up to a million dollars a week in your spare time? Just sell our product to all your neighbors and get them to sign up as representatives too."* He had fallen for one of those get-rich-quick-and-easy pyramid gimmicks when he was in college. He knew better now. By the time Joe had imagined all the worst-case scenarios, he was ready to throw the coupon away.

But something told him to keep it.

After all, he had a free cup of coffee or tea coming the next time he went to Mac's Place—*if* he went there again.

Now, as he sat at the conference table quietly listening to Amanda wow AguCo with the television campaign, Joe's mind played with the words on the back of the coupon.

Am I as rich as I want to be? Of course not! I need a lot more!

Suddenly Joe became aware of an embarrassing silence. No one was speaking, and all of his colleagues—and several of the AguCo representatives—were looking directly at him. He realized Amanda had finished her part of the presentation. It was his turn. *What am I supposed to be talking about? How could I have allowed my mind to wander like this? Think. Say something.*

"Uh, thanks, Amanda. That'll be some TV campaign, won't it?" As he struggled to form sensible words and phrases, he quickly rehearsed the presentation again in his mind to find his place. And he found it.

"Now, if you'll open the packet in front of you marked 'Campus Pranks,' we will look at the direct marketing plans we have developed." As he spoke, confidence crept back into his voice, focus to his eyes, and singleness of thought to his mind. Coffee coupons and get-rich schemes were pushed far from him. The room relaxed, Joe went strong to the finish, and AguCo had found its ad agency.

"Joe, that's wonderful!" Marcy reacted to the news of the successful presentation. The love of her life was on the verge of the greatest deal of his life. But as she questioned him about the details, Joe noticed that Marcy's recurring habit of looking past his eyes as she talked—almost looking over his shoulder, as if the real recipient of her words were positioned three feet behind him—had resurfaced.

Joe had tried his best to understand Marcy's inability to focus on him when they talked. Even when they were dating in college and would sit together in the snack shop talking, Joe often felt as though Marcy were building a relationship with the jukebox behind him.

Joe knew that Marcy had come from a family where the father was absent most of the time. And when he was home, he was often intoxicated. His physical blows were typically aimed at Marcy's mother, but the equally destructive verbal blows were reserved for Marcy and her younger brother. When Marcy was twelve, her father moved out. And later her mother had surgery to remove the scar—the one caused by a broken beer bottle. Marcy's scars weren't as easily removed. She kept them hidden, like a well-kept secret deep inside.

She felt so ashamed of the part she thought she had played in the breakup of the home, even though it wasn't her fault. And her shame resulted in a terribly low self-image. She just couldn't look people in the eyes.

It wasn't until they had been married for more than three years that Marcy would finally look Joe in the eyes when they talked.

Now, after nearly ten years together as husband and wife, she was back to her old ways.

"Well, it's not official yet," he continued rather grimly as he sorted through the mail in his hands. "The AguCo board still has to give its okay. And it's a pretty tough bunch—always worrying about the bottom line . . ."

Then he suddenly paused and threw the envelopes into the air. He grabbed Marcy by both arms.

"JUST KIDDING. WE GOT IT! WE GOT THE ACCOUNT!"

He grabbed Marcy in a bear hug and swung her around, "WE GOT THE AGUCO DEAL! YOUR LOVING HUSBAND HAS JUST LANDED THE BIGGEST DEAL IN HIS FIRM'S HISTORY!

"I BE BAD! I BE BAD!" Joe boasted, as he pumped a fist in the air—and Marcy tried to pretend that he wasn't acting like a junior higher.

"Yes, Joe, you're bad—but in a good sort of way."

Joe suddenly realized he was the only one at the victory party. Marcy's mood had drastically changed.

"What's wrong, honey?"

"I haven't had that great a day—not like yours at least."

Joe took Marcy's hands in his. "Tell me about it."

Marcy began a long and detailed description of the day on the medical-surgical wing of St. James Hospital where she worked as a nurse.

Every single patient reaction.

Every harsh word spoken by her coworkers.

Every tiring effort—Marcy didn't leave anything out.

Joe tried to listen politely, but he grew restless, and deep inside his agitation was beginning to boil. Marcy's complaints weren't new.

Thankfully, she had accepted a new schedule that enabled her to work three twelve-hour shifts a week and be paid for forty hours.

But the new schedule hadn't erased the old problems—too few staff, too many hours, too little pay. Joe hit the Replay button in his mind.

"Listen, Marcy." He tried to put the right amount of pathos into his voice and also tried (unsuccessfully) to take some of his own excitement out. "I know you've had a rotten day. Let's go out to eat tonight. We can celebrate the AguCo deal and . . . uh . . . help you relax after your hard day."

"No, Joe, I'm too tired," Marcy replied with unusual sadness. "You can go out if you want to. I'm going to take a bath and warm up some of that casserole we had last night."

Joe deflated like a popped balloon. The excitement he had brought home had suddenly rushed out of him, only to be replaced with a mixture of anger and disappointment. One of those monumental arguments was taking shape. One of those *barnburners*— one of those in-your-face, "You always" arguments. He just wasn't in the mood for it. Not tonight. Not after landing the biggest deal of his life.

"Okay, Marcy. But I really don't feel like casserole tonight. I think I'll go get some fish and chips." He hated fish. But Joe had to get out of the house, and fish was the first thing that came to his mind.

He started driving in the direction he knew best, the route he took to work each morning. He turned onto Skyline Drive, heading for the fish shop, but when he got there, he found it was closed. The note on the door said simply, "Death in family. Back tomorrow." Relieved that he didn't have to eat the dreaded fish, he settled instead for a fast-food hamburger and a milkshake. The food was good, but he still felt terrible.

Hoping that Marcy would go to bed if he stayed out awhile longer, Joe drove around aimlessly. Eventually he found himself on Ventura Street, passing the filling station where he had tried to get a cup of coffee that morning. The yellow police tape was still stretched around the property, and Joe noticed that with the parking lot empty of cars, several teens had decided it was as good a place as any for skateboarding.

Joe's thoughts wandered back to the rainy start to his day and his desire for coffee. The smiling face behind the carved-wood counter came to mind. The kind man who had given him a cup for free. He had asked him—*what was it? Oh yes*—to identify the flavor of the coffee. He had never tried those flavored coffees before. Coffee should just taste like coffee, but there was a terrific flavor to Mac's House Blend. He remembered that morning—drying himself in his office, sipping from the paper cup, and discovering that he liked the taste very much. It had reminded him of some other taste, something his mother used to make.

What did that coffee taste like?

He remembered. He could even smell the cobbler as he envisioned his mother carefully taking it out of the oven. He remembered that it was warm and gooey and had just the right balance of tartness and sweetness to it.

Blackberry. Mom's blackberry cobbler. That's the taste.

He smiled at the memories. *I wonder if Mac's Place is still open.*

Thankfully, it was. Joe pulled into the same space he had parked in that morning, but now, instead of racing the rain to the shop, he got out of the car and walked leisurely to the door. With Mac's towel in his hand, he entered and inhaled the rich coffee scent. Mac was just putting a chrome pot on the counter.

"Blackberries!" Joe almost shouted. "The coffee tasted like blackberries."

"Very good, Joe," Mac replied like a kindergarten teacher, a broad smile spreading over his face. "Most people don't have a sensitive enough palate to get that without some help. I take it you liked it?"

Joe handed the towel back to Mac. "Yes, it was good . . . no . . . *very* good."

"Glad you liked it. It's actually a blend of Kenyan and Hawaiian Kona coffees. I use the Kona as a base and mix in enough Kenyan to bring out the flavor. You must have an advanced set of taste buds."

Searching for something to say in response, Joe answered, "I guess I know what I like and what I don't like."

"How about another cup?"

"Sounds good to me, Mac. But I'm going to pay for this one."

"I'll be glad to let you—unless, of course, you want to use the coupon I gave you this morning."

Joe hadn't thought about the coupon, not since that embarrassing moment in his sales meeting. Now the puzzling words came rushing back to him. *Are you as rich as you want to be? Ask Mac.*

"No," he said. "I'll hang on to the coupon for another time. But let me ask you something." Joe didn't wait. "What does that saying on the back of this coupon really mean?"

CHAPTER 3

MARCY was probably asleep upstairs. Alone in the former basement—now a finished family room—Joe was overwhelmed by the almost deafening vacuum of sound. No television playing. No music on the stereo. He didn't even hear the faint but irritating sound of the bamboo wind chimes that hung on the deck. All he heard were the words Mac had spoken to him in front of the fireplace in the coffee shop—more than two hours before. Like a CD stuck on Repeat, Mac's words echoed over and over again in Joe's mind. It was as if Mac were sitting in this same darkened room. Joe played back the events:

"What does this mean, Mac?" Joe pointed to the words on the back of the coupon.

"Just what it says, Joe. Are you as rich as you want to be?"

"Of course not! People never get as much money as they want."

"This has very little to do with money, Joe. True riches seldom do, you know."

Joe remembered asking with a slight hint of accusation in his voice, "Is this one of those buy-real-estate-with-no-money-down things? I'm really not interested in that, to tell you the truth. I get it. You sell Mary Kay."

"Absolutely not, Joe. Nothing like that whatsoever."

"Not some multilevel marketing scheme?"

"Well," Mac hesitated. "I guess you could call it multilevel." He paused, seeming to be weighing his words. "Yes, it most definitely would be multilevel." Mac's face brightened. "Very good, Joe. I've never had it explained like that before."

Joe remembered his reaction.

"Well, Mac, I think I'd better just get a cup of coffee and be going. I'm really busy in my current job. I really don't have extra time to put into a business venture right now."

Mac shrugged—more to himself than anyone else. Reflecting on Joe's words, he took a large paper cup and directed Joe to a selection of chrome pots at the far end of the bar.

"These are our decafs, Joe. You might want to stay away from the caffeine this late in the evening—it might keep you awake. Try the decaf Sumatra. I think you'll like the hint of roasted nut in the flavoring."

"I had always thought decaf coffee was . . . well . . . flavorless," Joe replied apologetically, not wanting to admit that his knowledge of coffee was pretty much limited to "with" or "without" cream and sugar.

"On the contrary," replied Mac. "If processed correctly, decaffeinated coffees should taste just as good as regular coffees. The best processing plant is in Hamburg, Germany. That's where I get our beans processed. Then they're shipped directly to the private roasting house I use. The cup you're about to drink went through the decaf process this past Wednesday. It was roasted yesterday, and ground and brewed less than twenty minutes ago. If you were to sample the decaf Sumatra along with regular Sumatra, I doubt that even you, Joe, with your excellent palate, could tell the difference."

As Joe looked at Mac, the motherboard of his brain began processing. *This man doesn't appear to be a huckster. He really seems knowledgeable. Why, then, would I have a problem believing Mac could give me financial advice?*

"I'll try a cup of that, thanks." Joe reached for his wallet to pay for the coffee. "How much is it, please?"

"One dollar even," Mac said.

"Well, I know you'll never be as rich as you want to be only charging a buck for a large coffee. Even the gas stations charge more than that." Joe had expected the usual three to four dollars that the boutique coffee shops in Seattle charged.

"Joe, being rich has nothing to do with money. As a matter of fact, I became a richer man this morning by giving you that first cup of coffee."

Joe had nearly reached the door. He stopped and, with a puzzled look, turned to the coffee shop owner.

"Okay, Mac, just how did you get richer by giving me a cup of coffee?"

"It's simple," answered Mac with laughter in his voice. "Because when I met you this morning, I gained another friend."

⸺✺⸺

The day's events continued to replay.

The fire was dying, so Mac skillfully placed another log on the heap of coals and gave the pile a stir with the poker. By now Mac and Joe had taken seats in overstuffed leather chairs facing the fire, with their feet propped on a common footstool. Joe was sipping his decaf Sumatra; Mac was drinking plain tap water from his Seattle Mariners mug. Outside it had started to drizzle once again.

Curiosity, and a sense of confidence in this man he had just met that morning, caused Joe to pull out the coupon once again and ask Mac to explain more clearly what it meant.

"Joe, true riches, the things that really make a man wealthy, cannot be bought and sold. You can't buy them in a market or trade them as a commodity. You can't deposit them in the bank. And you won't hear commentaries about them on the financial news programs.

"Just the same, these *true* riches cannot be lost in a recession or a depression. As a matter of fact, in financial downturns, the real wealth I'm describing only increases in value. No, my friend, money is not wealth. Not real wealth anyway."

There was something in Mac's voice, in his eyes, that made Joe hunger to know what these "true riches" really were. It was as if Mac were a pirate and had shown Joe a secret map for finding buried treasure.

"Then what's this real wealth you're talking about?" Joe asked excitedly.

"If you really want to know, I'll share it with you. It won't come easily. It will seem hard to understand at times. And it will be even harder to apply in your life. It won't bring overnight results. As a matter of fact, it will take the rest of your life to acquire this wealth. Only after you're dead and gone will the vast holdings of your riches be evaluated.

"Having heard this, do you still want to know how to obtain true riches?"

Joe looked at Mac, astonished. Mac's eyes still had a dance in them, but his smile had been replaced with a look of utmost seriousness.

"Well, to tell you the truth—and I mean no disrespect—I mean, you really don't look rich. Do you have your treasure buried somewhere?" Joe added this last remark to make his comment sound less harsh, but Mac answered in a quiet voice that commanded Joe's entire attention.

"Joe, I have more wealth than you can possibly imagine—and more than I'll ever deserve. And I'm offering you the chance to gain your own treasure. Are you up for it?"

Joe could tell Mac was serious about this subject. He didn't know why, but the strength of Mac's conviction made it impossible for him to back out now.

"Yes, Mac, I want to know what you consider to be true riches."

Mac took a long sip of the water in his cup. He sat forward in his chair, pushed some rebel strands of hair back from his forehead, and looked straight into the eyes of the younger man seated before him.

He stared hard, as if looking for something in Joe's eyes. Then he relaxed, sat back, and smiled.

"Good. Then I'll be your teacher."

CHAPTER 4

"THERE was once a young man who had the world by the tail. He had his life mapped out, and his destination was the financial promised land."

Mac and Joe were alone in the coffee shop, the last customer having left just as Joe arrived. Mac had turned the sign in the window around to read "Closed." Joe helped upturn the chairs on the tables. Then they both took their seats in front of the fire. The rain had started again in earnest. Mac raised his voice slightly over the noise of the raindrops.

"This young man was fresh out of college in Texas and had moved to Seattle during the aeronautic manufacturing boom of the early seventies. He came as a stockbroker in search of gold. He used the old trick tried by a lot of brokers at that time. He selected a stock to watch, then sent out six hundred letters to prospective buyers, half of the letters saying the stock would rise in the next month, half saying it would fall. If, at the end of the month, the stock had risen, he would discard the names to which he had predicted it would fall. With the remaining 300 names, he selected another stock and did the same thing. The next month, using the 150 names that had received accurate forecasts, he repeated the exercise one more time. Now, he had 75 people who had received three correct stock predictions in a row.

"The young man then picked up the phone and called each of the 75, asking if he could set an appointment. From this batch he could count on thirty-five to forty appointments, and from these he would usually get at least 15 investors. He repeated this exercise monthly until he had almost 130 investors he was managing. Most of these were nickel-and-dimers, throwing maybe a hundred dollars a month into the market. But a few took it seriously, investing a thousand or more each month."

Mac slowly got up and put another log across the glowing coals. He prodded the coals with the poker until the new log was burning steadily.

"Our young man had it made. He bought a brand-new foreign sports car, rented an apartment with a view, spent like a drunken sailor. Then, faster than he could blink, it all came down. Boeing laid off nearly twenty thousand people, and Seattle went from the place to be to the place to flee. Do you remember the billboard someone put up on the freeway? 'Will the last person leaving Seattle please turn out the lights?'"

"I remember my dad telling me about those days," said Joe. "He was laid off at his accounting firm as part of the trickle-down from the Boeing layoffs." Joe thought about his dad and how he had worked two jobs just to make ends meet. It was partly this memory that drove Joe toward his financial goals. He wanted his wife and children—if they were to have any—to have all the things he never had.

"Well, your dad had a lot of company. Those were bleak days for our young man. The country entered a prolonged recession, and the stock market lost favor with investors. All but a handful of his clients sold out at a loss, and those who remained were not adding new money. His income went from high-flyin' to grounded in less than three months. He moved from his luxury apartment to subsidized housing."

"What about the sports car?" Joe asked.

"Repo'ed. On his last day of work, once the ax fell, he packed up his personal stuff in a cardboard box and walked out to the parking lot just in time to see the tow truck haul his car away.

"So, here we find our leading man—standing in the rain, no job, no severance, no car. Pitiful, isn't it?" Mac's eyes smiled as he said this.

"Well, Mac, I assume there's more to this story. And I imagine that it somehow has something to do with being as rich as you want to be."

"Joe, you're right." Mac laughed a rich, genuine laugh. He took a pull of the water in his mug and resumed his story.

"Our young man was walking down the sidewalk toward where he remembered seeing a bus stop. He was wondering what bus he was supposed to take and whether he had enough money in his pocket for the fare, when a car pulled alongside him. The driver rolled down the passenger window and called the young man's name. We'll call the driver Kenneth, and we'll give our young man the name Mac."

"I had already guessed that one," said Joe, with a laugh of his own. He was thoroughly enjoying this conversation. Had he stopped to think about it, he would have been hard-pressed to name the last time he had had so much fun just listening to someone else.

"Well," continued Mac, "Kenneth was one of the nickel-and-dime customers he had signed up. Mac remembered that Kenneth was also fresh out of college and thought he had something to do with Boeing.

"You see, I have to admit, I wasn't really that familiar with my clients. As long as their money came in each month, I rarely bothered to call them. I couldn't have cared less about their personal lives. That would have required time and energy I was spending on building my business. I was only interested in myself. These clients were just the means to my chosen end: a financial rainbow.

"But I recognized Kenneth. When I first met him, I knew there was something different about him. I called on him at his apartment, but he didn't really seem to care about my sales pitch. He said he would be glad to let me invest his money and told me if the investment paid off, he wanted the profit to go to some charity. He gave me the charity's address, signed the contract, then wanted to talk to me about me—where I was from, what I wanted out of life, that sort of thing! I was a little taken aback by this, but a client was a client, so I answered quickly and moved on.

"Now, at the lowest point in my life, here comes Kenneth. He pulled up next to me and asked if I needed a ride. I told him I was heading for the bus, but he insisted he could take me where I needed to go. So I climbed in his car—I remember he drove an AMC Pacer—maybe the ugliest car ever made." Mac and Joe shared a laugh as they recalled the teardrop-shaped car that never would have won a beauty contest. Joe thought again about his car. It was not exactly ugly, and it did start most every morning. Maybe it was time for a new car. Well, with the contract he signed today, why not?

"As Kenneth pulled away, he said he needed to see me anyway. He had been laid off from Boeing and would probably not be able to invest any more money in the market for a while. I told him my story, including the car being towed away and how I had no idea what I was going to do next. I didn't mean to tell him all that. It just came out so easily—Kenneth had this way of listening with his eyes.

"Anyway, he just smiled and said, 'Great. How would you like a job with long hours and low wages?' First, I just laughed, but he said he really did need some help in a venture he was just starting. I had no idea what it was, but I said I was open to just about anything. So as he drove, he told me that getting let go from the factory was the best thing that ever happened to him. Now he could do what he really wanted to do."

Joe listened as Mac described the storefront coffee bar Kenneth had just opened. It was sandwiched between a tattoo parlor and a shoe repair shop. Across the street was a combination sporting goods and camera store with bars on the inside of the windows.

"Remember, this was the 1970s, before the fascination with good coffees we have now. To most people back then, coffee was that dark, hot drink that boiled in a percolator all day and tasted like old oil.

"But Kenneth had served a two-year stint as a missionary in eastern Africa and had come back with the taste of Kenyan, Ethiopian, and Yemen coffees fresh on his tongue. He found an importer to get these beans, plus beans from Central and South America and Indonesia, to Seattle, and he found a roasting house that would prepare the beans just as he wanted. Now, the hard part was to get people to prefer his coffee over what they were used to.

"He brought me into this hole-in-the-wall storefront with two tables and a total of three chairs. Behind the counter was a girl with an infectious smile. Kenneth introduced her as his fiancée, Michelle. He told me this site was the best he could afford at the time, but you could tell he was content. He started telling me about the different beans he had at that time, looking up every few minutes to smile at Michelle. He talked with me as if I loved coffee as much as he did. And, to tell the truth, in those few moments I suppose I did fall in love with coffee.

"Kenneth told me he needed someone to work in the store in the evenings when he and Michelle were in class, and he also needed someone to take fliers advertising the coffee shop—each with a coupon for a free cup of coffee—to offices throughout the downtown area. The pay he offered was meager, but it was something when I was getting nothing. I asked how soon I could start."

Mac leaned forward and asked Joe, "I'm not boring you with this story, am I?"

"Not at all," said Joe. "But, well . . . I mean . . . couldn't you have moved to another town and started your business back up again? After all, it seems you had found a great way to get clients. You could still be making big bucks!"

Mac sat back in his chair and stared deep into the dying coals of the fire. Outside, big raindrops were still falling.

"Yes, I suppose so. Yes, I could have found another job, although you're right that I probably would have had to move. And I don't doubt I could have made a lot of money in the market. If I had done that, though, I would have missed out on the greatest reward I have ever had. Like I said earlier, Joe, it has nothing to do with money. My reward was learning the value of friendship. When I met Kenneth, I met a true friend. Up to that point in my life, I had been a hermit surrounded by people. I had lived a life of my own—my own thoughts, my own pursuits. I had worked so hard in college that I seldom took time to get to know those I lived with. And when I graduated, I set out to make my own way. Sure, I wanted to make a lot of money. I had a dream of owning yachts and fast cars. But I had never taken time to develop a deep relationship with someone else.

"Joe, a true friend is greater than any material possession. Aristotle said that without friends no one would choose to live, though he had all other worldly goods."

Joe sat silently and stared ahead. So this is what it was all about. Friendship. But why was this so important to Mac that he had it printed on the coupons he gave out? Mac resumed his story.

—∞∞—

SOMEONE WHO HAS MUCH MONEY BUT NO FRIENDS IS A POOR MAN INDEED.

—∞∞—

CHAPTER 5

"I COULD have continued on my career path as a broker," said Mac. "I'm sure I could have been a very good broker, as a matter of fact. And there's nothing wrong with working hard and gaining a good income. But if that's all there is in life, well, it now seems very empty to me."

Mac spoke of his beginnings in the coffee business. He poured himself into the different countries, and finally different estates in those countries. He suggested taking a thermos of hot coffee and paper cups to an office building and giving out free cups of coffee along with coupons. When the sky would open and deluge pedestrians with rain, as only the sky in Seattle can do, Mac and Kenneth would open the doors of their shop and offer shelter to as many as would fit. They would then pour everyone a sample cup of coffee for free. Soon word spread that not only could you get free coffee at K&M's Coffee Shop when it was raining, but the coffee itself was excellent.

"Business was great, and we were having a ball. But the thing I looked forward to the most was spending time with Kenneth. We talked about everything.

"Whenever I had a new idea or a new question, I couldn't wait to see Kenneth so we could talk about it. I had opened my heart to someone else and, in doing so, was seeing myself and the whole world around me in a brand-new way. Kenneth wasn't my only new friend. I was getting to know people in offices nearby, regular customers, even one elderly man who would stop by even if it was just sprinkling to ask if he could have a free cup. It became a daily pursuit of mine, finding someone new with whom to strike up a relationship.

"Now I felt accepted. I sensed I was more than just me, if you can understand what I mean. Joe, I felt like the richest person in the world."

Mac was best man at Kenneth and Michelle's wedding, worked double shifts at the coffee bar while the young couple took a short honeymoon, and later arranged a party at the store when Kenneth and Michelle each graduated from the community college. Within a year of his start in the coffee business, Mac was recognized by local coffee experts as someone with a very fine palate, someone who could not be fooled by a bad batch of beans. K&M quickly outgrew its first location; Kenneth and Mac scouted out and found a bigger site near The Market. Mac put in place a program where he installed coffee makers in local offices, then delivered coffee twice a week to those offices. Several restaurants began serving K&M coffee to their customers. Things could not have been better.

"Along the way I met a wonderful girl named Maggie, and we got married. Kenneth and Michelle had two kids before we had our first; then our son, Michael, was born. Our families did everything together.

"But best of all," said Mac, "was the relationship Kenneth and I had. We were tighter than this." He brought his hands together, with fingers closely interlocked. "He brought out the best in me, and I in him."

"Where's Kenneth now?" Joe asked. "Is he still around?"

"He's dead." Mac's hands had fallen apart. Now they lay lifeless on his lap. "He died last year from a heart attack. Michelle moved to Los Angeles to live with their oldest son. She's doing as well as can be expected."

They both sat quietly. The rain had all but stopped. The fire was dead. From the corner of his eye, Joe could see that Mac was crying.

Mac wrapped up the rest of his narrative quickly.

"Many years ago I bought into the company, so half of it was mine. After Kenneth's death I sold all the assets to one of the big chains. That provided enough money for Michelle to be comfortable for a long time. I'm not quite ready to retire, so I moved out here to the suburbs and opened Mac's Place.

"Joe, you wanted to know what I meant by that coupon. Well, all I can say is the friendships I have had, starting with Kenneth, have made me feel like the richest person in the world. I wonder if you have friendships that make you feel that way. Are you as rich as you want to be?"

CHAPTER 6

THE sky was turning a pale gray when Joe finally fell asleep, still sitting in the chair in the darkened family room. Mac's last words to him as he locked the door to the coffee shop echoed through Joe's mind until sleep was beginning to win over its adversary: curiosity.

I don't think I have anyone you would probably call a friend, Joe reflected. *I know a lot of people, but not like Mac was talking about.*

"I'd love to be your teacher, if you'd let me," Mac's words echoed in the almost empty room. "Come back when you can, and we'll start you on your own great adventure."

On the drive home from Mac's Place, Joe had sorted through the conversation as if he were searching for a file on his computer. He had always thought the empty feeling he had was some kind of inner motivation that drove him to business success and helped him reach his career and personal goals. But just a few miles down the road, Joe began to understand that this empty feeling was not from lack of status or money or anything material. The bone-dry, empty feeling came from something much deeper: It came from a part of him he rarely took time to explore. There was a hole in his soul. *Could it be there because I don't have any real friends?*

Two hours of sleep were five fewer than he was used to, but somehow Joe felt wide awake as he drove to work the next morning. He was alert as he met with his team to review the previous day's meeting with the AguCo marketing committee. Any drowsiness was forever erased when the signed AguCo contract was faxed to his office at half past ten. And he was positively hyperactive when Keith Stuart, the founder, owner, and president of Stuart Creative Media, came by to congratulate Joe personally and offered to take his whole team to lunch.

After lunch Joe crashed. He sat at his desk and stared at his computer screen for ten minutes, trying to shake the weary cobwebs out of his head. He headed down the hall for the less-than-tasty coffee from the machine that couldn't pour a cup without baptizing the linoleum underneath it.

"Hey, Joe," Kathy from Accounting greeted him as they met in the break room. "Great account you guys brought in."

"Thanks, Kathy," Joe replied, trying to keep a lid on his pride while he wiped the linoleum with paper towels. "Can I buy you a cup?"

"No, thanks," Kathy answered. "I just came down to get my yogurt. Late lunch."

Kathy grabbed her yogurt and a spoon and sat down at the table with some ads from the morning paper. Joe launched another attack on the coffee machine. This time he won. He tried to take a sip, but the coffee was way too hot, so he took it back to his office. Once it had cooled for a few minutes, he tried it again. The taste was totally unlike the coffee he had tasted the day before at Mac's Place. Had he really been drinking this horrible sludge for so long without noticing how bad it was?

Joe soon realized he wouldn't be much good to himself or to anyone else the way he felt right now, so he decided to leave. He told the receptionist he would check his voice mail from his cell phone, and he headed for the parking lot. As he maneuvered his way through the parking lot at the agency, he thought he might just stop by and get some *real* coffee from Mac.

All of the tables were full when he walked into Mac's Place. Most looked as if they were occupied by high-school students. Backpacks were unceremoniously scattered on the floor near the tables, and adolescent-filled chairs were pointing in all directions. The teens had drinks in front of them, many with a whipped-cream topping. They were loud, but not out of control. Mac was behind the counter washing cups, unbothered.

Joe moved toward the fireplace and stood, taking in the scene. The shop was teeming with energy, yet it was not overly noisy. Joe

watched as Mac finished drying the cups, then came out from behind the counter to talk with a teenage boy. The boy looked to be
about fifteen, skinny, with thick glasses. He was sitting by himself,
watching his classmates conversing with their friends. Mac pulled
up a chair and began talking with the boy. Joe couldn't hear their
conversation over the general din, but whatever Mac said to the boy
hit home. The boy sat more upright and soon began talking to Mac
with a look of excitement on his face. After a few moments Mac
looked up and, catching Joe's eye, waved and shouted a greeting.

"Hello, Mac," Joe yelled back. He felt better already. Somehow
just being in the room with all of the high-energy teens made him
more alert.

"Hiya, Joe. Be right with you." After a few more moments, two
other teens came in and made their way to Mac's table. After intro-
ductions were made, the two new teens opened their backpacks to
get out textbooks, and the three carried on their own conversation.
Mac made his exit and headed for the fireplace. He was still wearing the same khaki shorts, but today's off-white shirt had a maroon
stitched sketch of a coffee cup with steam rising from it.

"What can I get for you?"

"A *real* cup of coffee, please, Mac. Anything but that coffee-ma-
chine stuff." As they made their way to the counter, Joe complained
about the disappointing cup he had poured at work. Mac once again
complimented Joe on his discerning palate.

"You would make a good taster, Joe. You can tell what's good
from what isn't. Or, in your words, what's *real* and what's not."

Joe looked over the chrome pots available on the beautiful
counter and asked for a cup of Costa Rican La Miñata. While Mac
filled a cup and took Joe's dollar, Joe thought about their conversation the night before. And he remembered the empty feeling he had
experienced in the wee hours of the morning. As he reached for the
cup, he decided he would reach for something more.

"Mac, last night you spoke of relationships as if they were the most important thing in your life. Could we talk a little more about that?"

Mac's eyes sparkled as he replied, "Joe, I was hoping you'd stop by and ask me that. Yes, I'd be glad to share more about the power of relationships. But, as I warned you yesterday, the lessons may not be easy, and it may take your lifetime to see the results."

Joe instantly responded. "Mac, I just signed the biggest deal of my career. It made me feel really good—for a short time. But somehow it doesn't seem . . ." Joe's voice trailed off as he searched for words to describe what he was thinking.

"It doesn't seem real, Joe?" Mac finished the sentence. "Like the difference between the coffee at your office and the coffee here?"

"Yeah! That's it!" Joe took a long sip of his La Miñata. "This tastes like real coffee. The stuff at work was flat, tasteless—and very messy, I might add. Yet people drink that coffee all day long."

Mac chuckled. "That's the first lesson in friendship, Joe. Like coffee, real friendship is always good. It doesn't leave a bad taste in your mouth. It leaves you wanting more."

Joe answered the advice with a laugh. "Do you compare everything with coffee?" Mac joined in the laugh. Several of the students heard the loud laughter, but soon they were back sipping their lattes and whispering like church members during the offertory.

Mac continued, "Once again, your perception is impeccable. Let's use coffee as a basis for our lessons on relationships. You name the time, and we'll use Mac's Place as the classroom."

Joe thought for a minute and decided mornings would be the best time to meet. Things didn't usually start happening at the agency until at least half past nine, and the mornings Marcy worked, she left at six. Joe asked if eight o'clock was a good time.

"Great! That's right at the end of my morning rush. How about tomorrow?"

"Tomorrow it is, Mac. I'm not sure what we're going to talk about or where all this is going, but I have to say, I'm looking forward to it."

CHAPTER 7

JOE'S early enthusiasm for a new idea soon had a cloud hanging over it. *What have I gotten myself into?* The next morning as he was dressing, Joe was trying to figure out exactly why he was going to Mac's coffee shop again. *What do I need to learn about relationships? I know plenty of people and get along pretty well with most of them, thank you.*

Joe put his questions on the shelf next to that blue mouthwash and headed for Mac's Place. The morning's bright blue sky was like a quilted comforter over his confusion. He arrived a few minutes past eight, and there were only a handful of customers seated (including the three men who were regulars, all sitting with their leather books in front of them). But there were four customers waiting at the counter, fidgeting with cell phones in one hand and tired dollar bills in the other. Joe took a seat at a table with the morning paper and picked up the well-worn sports section to see how the Mariners were doing in spring training.

He had just finished an article that explained why the Mariners had no chance of winning their division without a solid closer when Mac approached.

"Sorry about the delay, Joe. A bit busier on the mornings when the sun is shining."

"No problem," Joe answered enthusiastically. "Can I get a cup of something kind of strong? The sun may be bright, but my eyes are still trying to break through the clouds."

Mac brought over a cup of his Breakfast Blend, along with another lesson.

"A lot of people mistake 'strong' for 'more caffeine,' thinking it will make them feel more awake. Actually, 'strong' is an aspect of coffee that refers to proper brewing. A strong coffee is one that is brewed correctly, with all its natural flavors coming through. A weak or thin coffee is underbrewed and lacks flavor. This Breakfast Blend, for example, has as much caffeine as any of our other coffees, but it has a milder flavor, which many people like in the morning."

Joe handed Mac four quarters, paused to inspect the rich coffee in his ceramic mug, and began to express his thoughts on friendship.

"Mac, about this friendship talk. I've been thinking about it and . . ."

"And you don't really see any need to be taught how to have friends, right?"

"I'm not saying that, Mac. I just don't understand how my having friends makes me rich. Yeah, I'll admit I really don't have any close friends. I know a lot of people, but I wouldn't call any of them good friends. I guess I just can't put friendships and riches in the same box."

"Tell you what," Mac answered. "I'll let you come to your own conclusions after we've met for a while. But somehow I can sense you already know the answer for yourself."

Mac paused for a moment. The look in Joe's eyes was the only answer Mac needed. "Will you commit to these morning talks for at least a month?"

"I don't think I can come every morning. To be quite honest, it was pretty rugged just getting here today."

Mac nodded his understanding and then got up briefly to wait on a couple—the man was wearing jogging pants and an Ivy League sweatshirt that was unsuccessfully hiding the results of an extra-layer chocolate cake. His trim wife was wearing a business suit. After the purchase, she poured two artificial sweeteners into a decaf. He sprinkled chocolate shavings into a chocolate mocha and stirred it with a cinnamon scone.

Mac returned to the table carrying his cup of water. "Okay, how about two days a week—Tuesdays and Thursdays? Can you pull yourself out of bed two days a week for a chance to become really wealthy?"

Joe smiled and took a sip of Breakfast Blend, breathing in the aroma just before he drank. It had a smooth, almost buttery consistency. Both the taste and the smell made the cup delicious. "Two days a week? Well, okay, I guess I can do that. When do we start?"

"How much time do you have this morning?"

Joe said that in order to be at the office on time, he'd have to leave in about thirty minutes.

Mac took a long drink from his water cup and began the short course. He sounded authoritative without being professorial or demeaning.

"Coffee," he started, "is not a single flavor. An orange has a specific chemical compound that gives it a unique, singular flavor. The same with herbs, such as basil and fennel. But coffee is a complex combination of chemical reactions that are constantly changing. A coffee's taste is affected by its various flavors and aromas. It's also affected by the personal experiences of the drinker. Tastes and smells stored in our memories can come alive when they meet with a familiar counterpart in a cup of coffee."

Joe remembered the taste and smell of his mother's blackberry cobbler that had come back to him the first time he tasted Mac's Kenya blend.

"Friendships are just like that," Mac reasoned. "They're a combination of various experiences and memories that each person brings to the relationship. Every time friends meet, there's a chemical reaction, if you will, that adds new dimensions to the friendship. Each person in the friendship is constantly growing and changing, which means the relationship will also grow and change."

Mac zeroed in, "Remember that strong cup of coffee you asked for this morning? Well, just as the strength of a cup of coffee depends on how it's brewed, so a relationship between two people can be strong or weak, depending on how each person has been prepared. By that I mean the experiences each person brings to the relationship."

"So the strongest friendships are those where the friends have the most in common?" Joe asked.

"Not necessarily," Mac replied. "Actually, those who have the most in common seldom become great friends. It takes variety to make a great cup of coffee—and a great friendship.

"No," Mac said as he took a deep drink from his mug, "the main ingredient for a great friendship is the right soil. And this is what I hope you take away from today's lesson, Joe."

"Soil?" Joe interrupted. "I thought we were talking about coffee."

CHAPTER 8

LIKE many who live in the Northwest, Joe considered himself an outdoorsy guy. He enjoyed camping, hiking, biking, and fishing—in moderation. When it came to his own home, he took pride in landscaping his yard with seasonal flowers and bushes. But he could honestly say he knew very little, if anything, about soil.

"It's just dirt to me."

Mac explained, "Oh no, Joe! Soil is much more than just dirt. Well, I suppose what I mean is this: Dirt is much more than just dirt. It's the life source of everything that grows within it. For instance, that cup of coffee you're drinking would taste much different if the mixture of nutrients in the soil weren't right. Coffee trees do best in soil that's rich in potash, nitrogen, and phosphoric acid. But just as important—more so, really—is how much water the soil gets and what it does with the water."

Mac knew his coffee facts by heart and shared them with obvious enthusiasm—without being pompous.

"The right soil needs to be loosely compacted in order to absorb the right amount of water and to let the excess drain away. If the soil is too firm, water won't make its way very far below the surface. If it's too loose, it will hold too much water. Too much water, and the base of the tree will grow thick—at the expense of the branches and, thus, the fruit. Of course, too little water, and the tree's growth will be stunted, making it susceptible to disease.

"So you see, Joe, the farmer has to constantly check the soil to make sure it has the proper nutrients and that it's tilled to the correct consistency. Otherwise, the coffee tree won't produce the fruit that ends up in your favorite coffee."

Joe frowned. "I understand how good soil is important to farmers, but what does it have to do with relationships?"

"Good question," Mac replied. "I can see how you might be puzzled. But there really is a connection between the two. Think of your heart or your soul—whatever you want to call the essence of you, the 'true you'—as your soil. If this soil is not properly tend-ed, all of your other relationships—your fruit, so to speak—will be affected; they will be either stunted or overgrown in the wrong places.

"You need to make sure you're in right relationship with your-self, Joe, before you can have good relationships with others."

Joe responded, "You mean you must first be a friend to yourself before you can be a friend to others?"

Mac raised his mug of water in a toast. "Congratulations."

Joe thought about the principle. It seemed very simple. But he had no idea how to gauge whether he was on friendly terms with himself. He shared his concern with Mac.

"Well, Joe, how do you feel about *you*? Do you like who you are right now?"

"I've always been one to think I can improve in just about every area of my life," Joe answered. "I have goals for improving myself physically, mentally, and spiritually. But I don't think I will ever ar-rive at the place where I'm happy with myself and won't ever need to grow anymore."

"Goals are very important, Joe. They keep our soil in proper balance. Remember, we don't want it to be so firm that the right amount of moisture can't get into us. For example, some people think that everything about them is bad. They can't allow water—that is, good thoughts about themselves—to penetrate their hearts. On the other hand, there are those whose soil is so loose that they think about themselves all the time. The trunk of that tree is big, but it doesn't bear fruit.

"The good soil of people's hearts allows them to accept them-selves as they are, knowing there are areas that need improvement, but also giving themselves time to make the improvements."

"Don't you think it sounds kind of selfish to be concerned with *liking* yourself?"

—∞—

LESSON 1

YOU MUST FIRST BE A FRIEND TO YOURSELF BEFORE YOU CAN BE A FRIEND TO OTHERS.

—∞—

"No, Joe," Mac replied. "Truly selfish people are those who *don't* like themselves. They usually act out their self-loathing by putting others down, always wanting their own way, and then, when they don't get it, taking their anger out on others.

"Those who are at peace with themselves seldom think of self. They have that area of their lives under control, and that gives them the freedom to develop relationships with others.

"Jesus Christ, the wisest man who ever lived, told us to love our neighbors as we love ourselves. You see, in order to have strong outward relationships, we must have a strong inward relationship. That's why it's so important for you to be on friendly terms with yourself before you start building friendships with others."

CHAPTER 9

———⟡———

THAT night after dinner, Marcy went to a continuing education seminar at the hospital. Joe washed up, grabbed his rain parka and hiking boots, pulled a book from the shelves in the living room, and pointed his car toward Crystal Mountain.

Joe walked a short distance from where he had parked and found a dry spot under a fir tree where he could look down on the blanket of city lights. The sunset was in its peaceful final breaths, casting orange and purple hues like a last act of kindness toward the undersides of the gathering clouds. Rain was threatening, but it wouldn't penetrate Joe's shelter. He pulled the book from one pocket and a small flashlight from another.

The book was old and almost tattered. It had a faded orange cover with an illustration showing one figure scowling at another who was holding a plate of ham and eggs. Dr. Seuss could not have known the impact his simple children's book would have on this child more than twenty-five years after his father gave it to him.

Joe reverently opened the cover and read the inscription: *To Joey, I hope these words make you smile. Love, Dad.*

Joe had read these words so often that the page on which they were written was barely attached to the binding. He received the classic on his seventh birthday, the last birthday he would ever share with his dad. Michael Conrad died several months later from the cancer that ravaged his body. Afterward, Joey found it very hard to smile, no matter how much Sam I Am encouraged him to try green eggs and ham.

Is this when I stopped liking myself? How big a part of my life was lost when Dad died?

Joe was not the introspective type. He didn't spend a lot of time trying to "find himself." But the lesson Mac shared that morning had stirred something inside Joe that he had tried to ignore for years. Did he really like who he was? When was the last time he had felt good about himself?

Joe remembered coming home from his first day in first grade. His dad found him crying in a corner of their garage. "No one wants to be my friend," he sobbed when his dad finally got him settled down enough to talk.

"Why, Joey, I'm sure there are a lot of classmates who want to be your friend."

"No, they don't." The tears were starting to well up again. "No one even talked to me or played with me at recess."

Michael Conrad picked up his son and held him on his lap. "Joey, in no time at all you'll have lots of friends in your school. You're a great boy and you'll be a great friend. Son, if I were your age, I would want you as my best friend.

"And, Joey, I'll bet if you were someone else, you would want to be friends with Joey Conrad too."

Joe could almost smell the flannel material of his father's shirt. The memory of burying his sobs in his father's strong chest as he held Joe on his lap was as vivid as yesterday's lunch. He remembered continuing to cry, this time from relief that he did have a friend he could count on.

When his father died, he had no other male in his family to look up to. His mother did the best she could to be both parents to Joe and his older sister, Rachel. But Joe never again had someone like his dad to be his best friend.

Joe thought about his father's words to him that evening so long ago. Were they still true? *Yes, I believe if Dad were still alive, he would still be my best friend. But what about the second part? Would someone else want to be friends with Joe Conrad?*

Joe took a quick inner inventory, trying to be realistic in his self-assessment. Sure, he had faults, but who didn't? He felt that he also had a lot of positive qualities. He was faithful to his wife, he worked hard, he didn't cheat on his taxes. *But there has to be some-*

thing more than just being a nice person. What was it Mac said? The soil had to be the right consistency.

How is my soil? Is it so firmly packed that I'm overly severe with my-self? Or is it so loose that I think of myself too much? Joe reached down and grabbed a handful of the rich humus he was sitting on. He squeezed it in his fist, then released. The dirt held together firmly in his hand, but when he pressed his thumb into the ball, it crumbled easily. Here was soil that was just the right texture—firm, but not overly so. *Look at the beautiful things that have grown in this ground,* he thought. *Firs, pines, wildflowers—all of them got their nutrients from this soil that seems to be at peace with itself.*

Joe made a decision as he stared into the silver star-filled sky. He stood and wiped his hands on the sides of his denim jeans. He gathered up his worn book and walked back to his car, confident that he could make friends. He was going to start right now. And he was going to be friends with himself first.

CHAPTER 10

FOR the first time in recent memory, Joe found himself looking forward to the start of the week more than the weekend. He had spent so many Saturdays in his office on the AguCo account that it never felt like a weekend. Alex Redding from Accounting was there on Saturday as well. He was known more for arriving late and leaving early during the week than he was for working on Saturdays. Joe was too absorbed in his work to think much about it.

On Sunday Joe painted the guest room. Marcy had been after him for months to do the painting. First, he had to borrow a stepladder from Al Simpkins next door. *When was the last time I saw Al? He seems thinner.*

By the time Marcy got home from her shift at the hospital, Joe was putting the paint and brushes away. He knew she would be pleased with his work. Emotionally and physically exhausted, she just said it looked darker on the paint samples at the store than it did on their walls. After a microwave dinner, he went right to bed.

Monday was a marathon meeting with Creative and Placement to go over their roles in the AguCo campaign. During lunch, Joe tried striking up a conversation with D'Juan, but he seemed more interested in talking with Leslie. Joe felt somewhat left out of the lunchroom conversation—not just with D'Juan, but with everyone. He was older than all the other team members, and he was their boss. Was this why they weren't sharing their excitement from the weekend with him? He was really looking forward to his Tuesday morning lesson from Mac just for the company.

"Joe, it sounds like your mountaintop experience really produced a breakthrough! I appreciate your sharing that with me, especially the part about how much your father meant to you. I'm sure he was a very special man."

Joe was drinking Mac's Blend. He really liked the Kenyan part of the blend that had a berry flavor to it.

"Mac, I felt like I left a part of me on Crystal Mountain that night. A part of me that, well, has been very heavy. I felt like flying down the mountain."

"What happened then?" Mac quizzed. "When you came in here this morning, you said, 'It doesn't work.' What were you expecting to happen?"

Joe traced the cracks in the wood floor. "I thought when I started liking myself, Mac, that it would be easy to make friends. But I still feel like a leftover croissant from your bakery shelf. Shouldn't I have made at least one friend by now?"

Mac took a pull of his water. "Time for lesson number two. This one's pretty simple: In order to *have* friends, you must first *become* a friend."

Joe looked at Mac as if he had just explained a Nobel Prize–winning mathematical equation . . . in Greek.

"May be simple for you, Mac, but I don't get it."

"Too many people sit around waiting for the phone to ring. They wait for the other person to make the first move. There are lots of lonely people out there, Joe, and they all want friends. But those same folks should be out planting friendship seeds."

LESSON 2

IN ORDER TO HAVE FRIENDS, YOU MUST FIRST BECOME A FRIEND.

Mac got up and refilled Joe's cup, this time from a pot labeled Kenya Nyanja. "Try this. It's from a new batch of beans that just arrived yesterday."

Joe took a cautious sip. It had a pleasant smell and an even better taste.

"I'd say it tastes a bit like berries. Are you mixing berries with coffee beans now, Mac?"

"No," laughed Mac. "That's just your excellent palate at work again, Joe. Kenya coffees have a fruitiness that can come across like a berry flavor, such as the Kenya Nyeri I use for Mac's Blend, or more of a citrus flavor as in the Nyanja. The point is, in order to get a coffee tree to grow in the Nyanja estate in Kenya, a farmer had to plant the seed of a coffee tree. We can't harvest coffee if we don't plant coffee seeds. In the same way, you can't harvest friends if you don't plant seeds of friendship."

"Okay, Mac. Just what do these friendship seeds look like?"

"Hah!" Mac released a single laugh, almost like a big breath. "Well, you can't get them at the nursery, and you can't order them from a catalog." Mac had a laugh that drew others to him like flies to a picnic. The men seated at a nearby table—the ones who seemed to be there every morning with their black books—stopped what they were doing and looked in Mac's and Joe's direction.

"You plant these seeds by committing intentional acts of friendship. For instance, you mentioned your neighbor, Al. Let's start with him. A good way to become friends with someone is to do something kind for him or her. Can you think of something you could do for Al that would say, 'You matter to me'?"

Joe thought. "He did mention the reason he hasn't cut his lawn in two weeks is because his mower quit on him and he hasn't had time to take it to the shop."

"There you go." Mac smiled. "Offer to let Al use your mower until his is fixed. Better yet, why not cut his lawn for him?"

"I was afraid you might mention that." Joe groaned. "But I guess I could do it when I cut our grass this week. Neither of our yards is very big—it won't take that long."

"Good, Joe. And you could plant another seed of friendship by showing him you're interested in the things he's interested in. Do you know what Al likes to do?"

"I honestly have no idea," Joe confessed. He thought for a moment, then said, "I think he jogs. He used to be kind of heavy. I noticed he has lost weight—and I think I've seen him out running in the evenings."

"Another good idea. When you take his ladder back, ask him about something that relates to jogging."

"Now you've hit on a sore point, Mac. I need to lose some pounds myself. So I guess I should ask him for some pointers on getting started."

"Better yet, Joe, why not ask if you could go with him sometime? You're more likely to follow through with a commitment if you have someone holding you accountable. And this would be a great way to plant a seed of friendship."

"All right, Mac, but I wish we could think of a less strenuous way to start. I've been doing a lot of painting, you know."

CHAPTER 11

AS THE sun took its last bow, Joe picked up his pace to finish mowing the last three rows of grass in the two backyards. He thought it might be faster if he cut his yard and Al's at the same time—in effect, thinking of them as one big yard. Joe always liked cutting grass. He liked the immediacy of the results: One minute the grass is long and shaggy, the next it is short and neatly trimmed.

Maybe I should have been a barber, he thought.

Al arrived home just as he was finishing up. Joe stopped the mower long enough to explain that as long as he was already doing his lawn, why not one more? At first, Al hesitated. Joe even wondered if Al was angry. After a few awkward seconds, he simply said, "Thanks, Joe, that's very nice of you," and went inside.

Okay, I'm planting this seed. How long does it take to grow?

When Joe had finished cleaning off his mower and stowing it in the garage, he walked next door with Al's ladder in his hand. Al was sitting on his front porch sipping from a can of cola. Another unopened can was in his hand.

"Here's your ladder, Al. Thanks again."

"Joe, you really didn't have to cut my lawn. But thanks for doing it." He extended the cold can to Joe.

Taking the can, Joe responded, "No problem. Like I said, as long as I was doing mine, it was no trouble to cut another one right next door. By the way, you're welcome to use my mower any time you like."

Al said thanks again, drained the last of his drink, and looked away almost distantly.

"Al, I notice you've been jogging in the evenings. How far do you run?"

Al brightened noticeably at this turn in the conversation. He told Joe he had just started running again after about a ten-year hiatus. He was up to two miles a night and thought he could be at five miles by summer. Not only was he happy with his distance, but his time was improving as well.

"Wow," Joe reacted. "If I tried to run five miles, you'd have to time me with a calendar." They both laughed.

"Why not join me, Joe? You'd get in shape in no time."

"I bet I would," said Joe. "But I haven't jogged in a long time. I would just slow you down."

"Hey, I'm not that fast. Want to go for a short jog right now? Say half a mile. That would be a nice distance to start with. And since this is my night off, I won't feel like I have to push it."

Joe agreed reluctantly, considering his tired muscles.

Al showed Joe his stretching routine, then they started off on a leisurely run. At least at this pace it would be easy to carry on a conversation.

"I've noticed you running more often, Al. Are you training for a race or just wanting to get in shape?"

"Well, actually, I have a lot more time on my hands these days. I got laid off from my job last month."

Joe tried to remember where Al had worked or even what line of work he was in. It just wasn't coming to him, so he chose a neutral route.

"That's a bummer," Joe shook his head. "Is there a general downturn in your industry or is it just your employer?" He hoped he sounded sincere—at least as sincere as one could while gasping for breath.

"No—I got let go because, well, I haven't told anyone else this, but what could it hurt? I got fired for being drunk on the job. And alcoholic bankers aren't in much demand right now. So I don't know when I'll get another job."

They had circled the block—Al said it was half a mile—and were back on Al's porch. Joe was sweating and holding his side.

Al looked as if he had walked to the mailbox and back. "I started drinking to relieve the stress of the day. Then I started drinking because it felt good. Finally, I was drinking because I had to. I hate myself when I drink, and I hate the feeling when I don't drink.

"The worst part for me isn't the lack of a job. It's the loneliness. Most of the guys at the bank hang out together after work and on the weekends. Now, they act like I don't even exist. This is the first conversation I've had of any length in more than two weeks. Thanks for coming over, Joe."

"Sure. I'm sorry all that's happened. And I'm sorry I didn't know about it sooner. I guess I haven't been much of a neighbor."

"I wouldn't know, Joe. I've been drunk the better part of two years now." Al's voice started to quiver—tears flowed freely down his face. "And I have no idea what I'm going to do now."

Joe first wondered, *What would Mac do in this situation?* He remembered lesson two: In order to have friends, you have to be a friend. What do friends do? Friends help those who can't help themselves.

"Al, have you tried Alcoholics Anonymous? I hear they're real good at helping people." This was the extent of Joe's knowledge of AA, but it was better than nothing.

"Yeah, I even called and found a group that meets near here. I guess I'm just too chicken to go. I mean, I don't know anyone there. What'll I say?"

Joe quickly answered, knowing the longer he thought about it, the less likely he would do what he should.

"When's the next meeting?"

"Well," Al said, "there's one tomorrow evening. I had thought of going, but . . ."

"Just give me a call and I'll go with you," Joe offered.

The next night the meeting went extremely well. When Joe returned home it was nearly midnight. He said goodnight to Al and promised he would go to another meeting with him in two nights. They also traded phone numbers. Later, Joe crawled into bed with the most satisfied feeling he had known in a long time.

CHAPTER 12

WHEN Joe had finished telling Mac about the time he spent with Al—about the jog, about their conversation, about the AA meeting they had attended—Mac looked like a father whose son had just presented him with a straight-A report card.

"Joe, I believe you're a richer person this week than you were last week. And I daresay Al is as well."

"You're right, Mac. I felt great when I was able to help Al last night. I think we just might become good friends."

"I think you already have, Joe."

Joe sipped from a paper cup of Breakfast Blend. "What's today's lesson?"

Mac was wiping down the counter with a damp cloth. "I'm afraid I'll have to postpone today's lesson, Joe. I have a doctor's appointment this morning and have to close up for a while. But if you can spare some time this evening, I'd like to take you on a field trip."

Joe asked if everything was okay. Mac answered, "Just some tests. You know how doctors like to overdo things."

They said good-bye.

At seven that evening, Joe pulled into Mac's parking lot and slogged through a downpour into the coffee shop. It was empty and the chairs were already upturned on the tables. Mac was washing up a chrome pot.

"Towel, please," Joe yelled, and then caught the towel tossed to him.

"Turn that sign around so it says 'Closed,' will you please, Joe?" Mac wiped his hands on his own towel that was draped from his belt, then reached back to turn off the lights. "Follow me out back to my car."

They drove through the heavy rain, with windshield wipers whipping back and forth like maniacal metronomes. Mac headed back toward the city, exiting in a light industrial area that Joe had seen from the highway but never had reason to visit.

"Joe, I thought you might like to see where I get my coffee roasted. This particular roaster has a very loyal following, mostly outside of Seattle. He roasts in small batches only, and I would put his roasts against any in the city. He's done this now for nearly thirty years. I think you'll like Jim."

Jim Mathis was shorter than both of the visitors and much rounder as well. He wore tattered denim cutoffs, a Grateful Dead T-shirt, and designer basketball shoes that were nearing retirement. He greeted his visitors at the back door marked "Pick Up Orders in Front 9-5." It was nearly eight.

"Mac's the only person I allow in here after hours," Jim said as he grasped Joe's hand and squeezed it like a lemon. "And I doubt he even knows where the front door is."

Jim was the kind of person you take to instantly. His smile and laughter were sincere and inviting. Joe could feel good things were in store.

Mac told the story of how he and Jim met at Mac's first store in the heart of a seedy downtown retail district. Jim had come by initially to try to get Mac to use his roasting services. After sampling Jim's beans for a few weeks and deciding the consistency was excellent, Mac had agreed to buy his beans from Jim. He concluded his almost formal comments to Joe by saying that he was a very wealthy man indeed for having known Jim for more than twenty years. Jim's smile grew even wider.

They toured the roasting facilities, with Jim bragging on different machines as if they were his children. He had three identical main roasters clustered together in the middle of the largest room.

"The coffee roaster really hasn't changed in more than sixty years," Jim explained. "No need to change it. It's really just a big steel drum that turns over and over. The beans are heated by these gas jets here."

Joe pointed to a rod that was pushed into the end of each machine. "What does that do?"

Jim pulled at one of the rods until it came out. At the end was a large spoon with its end pointed up. "We use this to check the progress of the beans while they're roasting. It's called a 'tryer.'"

Jim led them to a smaller room that was packed floor to ceiling with burlap bags. The door closed firmly behind them, keeping the climate-controlled room in a constant temperature and humidity range. The air was filled with a smell reminiscent of sweet alfalfa.

"This is our green room," he said, smiling. "A green room in a theatre or TV studio is where the performers go to prepare just before they go onstage or in front of the camera. This is where the coffee beans go just before they're turned into the coffee we drink."

He opened the throat of one of the bags and pulled out a handful of what looked like large split peas.

"If you grind these beans and place them in boiling water, they would bear absolutely no resemblance to any type of coffee. They have the right chemicals within them to create incredible flavors, but it takes someone with the know-how to bring those flavors out. You might say I have to encourage the flavors to come out." Jim winked and grinned at Mac.

"So there's a real science to this roasting, huh?" Joe asked.

"Well, more art than science. A true roaster knows how each bean was grown and the potential flavors it has. Then, the roasting process has to be timed just right so those flavors will be locked in the bean until it's ground for brewing. If the beans are in the roaster for too short a time, they'll taste sour when brewed. Too long and they'll have a burnt taste. Yes, I guess science does enter into the process, but I think of myself more as an artist than a scientist."

Jim gave Joe an airtight bag of roasted beans. "These little guys are from the Volcan Baru region in Panama. I think you'll be surprised at the bright flavor this coffee has."

Joe thanked him for the coffee and the tour as he and Mac climbed back into the car. Back on the interstate, Joe remarked on how much he enjoyed meeting Jim.

"Joe, I wanted you to meet him for more than just some tips on roasting. Jim really was teaching you lesson three."

Joe smiled and said, "I thought there might be something more to this little field trip. I noticed the look he gave you when he was talking about encouraging the flavors to come out of beans."

Mac chuckled. "Very little gets past you, Joe. Yes, tonight's lesson is on encouragement. How can you apply what you learned about roasting green coffee beans to relationships in your life?"

Joe sat in silence for a few minutes, then said hesitatingly, "I suppose people are like the green coffee beans. Those beans have flavor in them, but there has to be a chemical reaction to bring it out."

"Very good, Joe. Now, what do you think that chemical reaction is that brings out the 'delicious flavor' each person has inside?"

"I think Jim gave it away with the word *encourage*. Is that it?"

LESSON 3

IF YOU MAKE ENCOURAGING OTHERS A DAILY HABIT, YOU WILL NOT WANT FOR FRIENDS, AND YOU'LL FEEL GOOD ABOUT LIFE.

"Bingo. This is so exciting, Joe. You and I get to play a very important role in our friends' lives. We have each been given a very powerful tool to use in bringing out the best in others—our words.

With every person we meet, we choose how we want to use this tool. In fact, when we use our words for good, we make a positive difference not only in the life of the hearer but in ours as well.

"Every day we should look for someone to encourage. It might be a simple comment to a clerk at the gas station, a thank-you note, or a positive e-mail to a colleague. But I guarantee two things: If you make this a daily habit, you will not want for friends, and you'll feel good about life."

Joe thought about the lesson, sitting silently as they threaded their way back toward Mac's Place. "This is so simple," Joe reflected aloud. "I expected some deep, involved theory. So, all I have to do is say nice things to other people . . . and mean it, of course?"

"Yes, Joe, it's really that simple. Give it a try for the next two days and let me know the results."

CHAPTER 13

UP TO this point, Joe hadn't been thinking about *immediate* results from the lessons on relationships. He thought it would be more of a lifelong pursuit. But the next morning as he dressed for work, he determined to try Mac's suggestion. He would make a game of seeing how many people he could encourage today.

As he stepped out of the bedroom, he found his first "victim."

"Morning, Marcy. You sure look good today. I really like your new hairstyle." It was the best he could do that early with his wife standing in the hallway without a trace of makeup on and wearing her grandmother's hand-me-down flannel nightgown. Marcy tried to compute Joe's remarks but could do no better than mumble her thanks as she headed back to bed with the morning paper.

Oh, well, it was a try at least. He had the rest of the day to improve on his "strokes."

He pulled into his parking space just as Alex Redding from Accounting was getting out of his car. Joe had never talked much with Alex. He seemed to be rather distant with most everyone at work. But this seemed like as good a time as any to get to know him.

"Nice car, Alex." Joe nodded toward the SUV. "How do you like it?"

Redding looked at Joe as if he were a complete stranger. "It's fine. It's my wife's." With that he simply continued toward the lobby.

Two for two. At least I'm consistent, Joe mused.

As he entered the elevator, Maria Alicia stepped in. She had a pained expression on her usually bright face.

"Morning, Maria Alicia. Are you all right?"

The young Venezuelan looked at her boss and winced. "Just a little sick this morning. But it's a good sick. I'm pregnant."

"That's great, Maria Alicia." Joe had gone to her wedding last year. *Now what is her husband's name? Oh yes.* "What does Jake think? Is he excited?"

"Is he! He wants a boy. All I want is to keep my breakfast down."

Words. Joe suddenly needed some encouraging words.

"Well, Maria Alicia, I'm sure you're going to make a great mom. You already have that mother's glow about you."

This seemed to help the queasy mother-to-be. She turned to Joe as they stepped off the elevator.

"Thanks. I really needed that, especially this morning."

Joe felt something go through him like a jolt of electricity. He had simply said something nice to this young woman, and it obviously pleased her. It made him feel good as well.

As they walked toward the office, he continued, "I'll tell you what, Maria Alicia. If it would help, you can come in a little later in the mornings until you get to feeling better. We've been putting in some late hours anyway—I have no doubt you'll get your work done."

She stopped and grabbed Joe's arm. "Oh, thank you so much. I was praying this morning that you might allow me to do that. I'm usually better by nine-thirty or ten. I'll make sure I get all my work done. I haven't been going out for lunch—I just eat crackers at my desk. Thank you, thank you."

Joe felt refreshed and energized by her gratitude. *There really is something to this encouragement thing.* He looked for someone else.

He passed Mr. Stuart in the kitchen area. "Morning, Mr. Stuart. Say, I just wanted to let you know we really appreciate all the help you've given us on this AguCo account."

Stuart looked at his employee with first a quizzical, then a pleased expression. "You're the one to be thanked, Joe. You and your team are doing a splendid job. By the way, are you free for lunch today?"

By the time he pointed his minivan toward home, Joe had counted fifteen different people—including Alex Redding and Marcy—whom he had offered encouraging words to. He didn't count their responses. After the first few opportunities, he found that by sharing kind words with others he had made *himself* feel better as well. The other person's response really wasn't important. However, most did respond in kind. As he drove home Joe knew he had increased his personal-relationship bank account greatly that day.

CHAPTER 14

"JOE, this morning I want to teach you how to 'cup' coffee."

Mac was dressed in his customary shorts, T-shirt, and sandals. He looked somewhat paler than usual, and it seemed to Joe that Mac was moving a bit slower than he should be. *Well, doesn't everyone move slower this early in the morning? Or could it be that there's something wrong with Mac?*

"You want to teach me to do what to a cup of coffee?" Joe asked.

"I want to teach you to 'cup' coffee. It's a way to test a batch of coffee, to determine its qualities. Come out back and I'll show you."

The shop was unusually empty, except for a few regulars who were seated at their usual places. Joe and Mac went through a single door to a small back room. In one corner was a sink. On the counter to the right of the sink was a small microwave oven; to the left were six small white teacups, with two silver spoons next to them. There was a pad of paper and a pen next to the cups.

"What I'm about to show you normally takes years to learn. But somehow, Joe, I suspect you'll pick this up quickly. You have a fine palate when it comes to tasting coffees. Now, let's see what you've been tasting."

While he was talking, Mac had placed a ceramic pitcher of water in the microwave and set the power on high. While the pitcher was warming, he took a bag of beans marked "S. Kalosi," scooped out two tablespoons, and put them in a small grinder. After twelve seconds of grinding—Mac looked at a big clock with a sweeping second hand just above the sink—he used the spoon to put the ground coffee evenly into two cups. He repeated this process with beans marked "N.G." and "Antigua." He then removed the ceramic pitcher from the microwave. Joe could see that the water was boiling hot. Mac poured water into each cup, filling them almost to the top.

"Now what?" Joe asked, genuinely excited.

Mac handed a spoon to Joe and said, "Let's start with the first cup, the Sulawesi Kalosi. This coffee is grown in an area of Sulawesi called Torajaland. The people of the region grow their coffee trees in their yards; the whole family takes part in the cultivation and harvest of the coffee. It's somewhat hard to get, so when I can buy it, I usually do.

"What we're going to do is try to distinguish its unique characteristics. I want you to listen to the coffee—hear what it's saying to you. Use the paper to write down your impressions. Try to be very specific in your descriptions. First, you'll listen with your nose, then your mouth. Any questions?"

Only a million, thought Joe. "What do you mean by 'listen to the coffee'? How do I listen to a taste?"

Mac smiled his warm, sincere smile, as if he had been waiting for this question all morning.

"Listening is much more than just hearing sounds. Listening involves all of your senses, being aware of what you see, feel, taste, and smell as well as hear. And, by the way, this is the next lesson in building great relationships. Become a good listener, and you'll never lack for friends."

Joe thought about the next principle. When he had had that neighborly talk on Al's front porch, Joe had listened. Just being available to listen seemed to give Al the opportunity he had been waiting for, the chance to open up and tell someone about what was destroying him on the inside.

"I think I'm a good listener at times, Mac. But other times I tend to do all the talking and don't give the other person a chance."

"Well, that's a good observation, Joe. You've heard the expression 'God gave us two ears and only one mouth,' so the conclusion is that we should talk only half as much as we listen. But remember that listening involves more than just hearing sounds. You'll need to learn to listen with all your senses. Let's try listening to this coffee. First, we'll test the aroma. Do what I do."

Mac picked up one of the teaspoons, and leaning down until his nose was almost in the cup, placed the back of the spoon on the crust that had formed on the top of the liquid and gently pushed it down. As he did, he breathed in deeply several times, then slowly stood up. Joe saw that his eyes were closed.

"Try that with your cup of Kalosi and write down what you smell."

Joe did—and he splattered some of the coffee on the tip of his nose when he broke the crust. The first words that came to his mind were a bit surprising, especially related to coffee. He wrote, "It smells like I'm in the woods right after a rain."

Next, Mac turned his spoon over and dipped it in the cup. Lifting the coffee to his lips, he slurped it loudly, like someone trying to annoy others while eating soup. Instead of swallowing, however, Mac spit the coffee out into the sink.

"You have to slurp it like that in order to spray the liquid over all of your taste buds. Try it."

Joe slurped his spoonful and once again recorded his thoughts on paper: "Tastes like nuts. Kind of spicy."

Mac and Joe repeated their procedures with the New Guinea and Guatemalan Antigua coffees. When they were finished, Mac quizzed Joe on his impressions.

"Which one tasted almost like butter?"

"New Guinea."

"Did one have a chocolate undertone?"

"Yes, the Antigua."

"Which one impressed you as being earthy?"

"Definitely the Kalosi."

Mac then took Joe's paper and examined it, nodding his approval as he read. "You have a gift; you really do. It takes most people years to be able to make these distinctions. Are you sure you haven't studied coffee?"

"Nope." Joe laughed. "You're just a great teacher."

They washed out the cups and spoons, then they returned to the front of the store. Joe paused to pour a cup of Mac's Blend in a paper cup—leaving a dollar next to the register—and turned to see Mac slowly making his way to the big, stuffed leather chair near the fireplace.

"Are you feeling okay, Mac?"

"Huh? Oh, sure. I didn't get much sleep last night. How did you like your first experience at cupping?"

LESSON 4

IF YOU LEARN THE ART OF LISTENING WITH ALL OF YOUR SENSES, YOU'LL NEVER LACK FOR FRIENDS.

"I loved it. It's a lot more exciting than trying to figure out what TV shows to advertise a fast-food chain on. But tell me, how can I become a better listener? I mean, how can I use listening to build friendships?"

Mac stared at the fire as he spoke. "This morning you told those cups of coffee you were interested in them. You shut out all other thoughts, all other interests, and gave each cup your full attention. You put your nose right down to that cup and allowed it to breathe on you. You took its essence into your mouth, at that moment, spraying it around to block out all other tastes so you could know only its uniqueness. You really *listened* to the coffee.

"When you're with people, you need to do the same thing. First of all, listen to them with your eyes. Don't let your eyes wander. That will tell the person that he or she is boring you. Second, listen with your body. Don't fidget as if you would rather be somewhere else. And then, listen with your tongue. Keep it still. When you listen like that, you'll be amazed at how others will seek you out, how they will open up to you. If you learn the art of listening with all of your senses—just like you learned the art of cupping this morning—you'll never lack for friends."

CHAPTER 15

BOB Service was the stereotypical accountant, Joe observed. Short, balding, dressed in a button-down blue shirt with a red print tie. Joe hadn't noticed, but he bet that Bob was also wearing wingtips. Bob was an accountant with the AguCo branch in Seattle and was visiting Stuart Creative to make sure actual costs were in line with estimates. He and Joe had just ordered lunch at a nearby chain restaurant, and Joe was already regretting not having invited another member of his team to go with them.

What do I say for a whole lunch hour to a person I don't know? I have nothing in common with this man. Why did I have to be the one to take him to lunch? Why not Alex Redding, our annoying senior accountant?

The waitress arrived with drinks: unsweetened iced tea for Joe and decaf coffee for Bob. As she placed the coffee in front of Bob, the cup passed under Joe's nose, and he caught the aroma. It smelled a bit like burnt wood that's been doused with water. The smell triggered his lesson from Mac earlier that morning. *Now is as good a time as any to practice being a listener.*

"So tell me, Bob, how long have you been with AguCo?" It was the best Joe could come up with.

"About three years," replied the accountant. Then awkward silence.

Great. And the appetizer isn't even here yet.

"Where did you go to school?" He tried to remember what Mac had said. Listen with the eyes; listen with the body. He looked straight at Bob, ignoring the new waitress passing by their table.

"Uh. I'm a Husky."

Well, that's two sentences. We're making progress.

"Did you major in accounting?"

Bob sipped his coffee before replying, wrinkling his nose slightly.

Yep, burnt wood, thought Joe.

"Well, that's what I got my degree in. But I started off in social work."

"My, that's quite a jump from social work to accounting. Why the switch?"

Bob began to tell him about growing up in foster homes after his mother had been arrested for possession of heroin. He never met his father. Bob was shuttled from home to home—some better than others—before he finally settled in the home of an elderly couple. They cared for him from the time he was ten years old.

"They loved me just like I was their own child. They never had any children of their own, so in a very real sense, I was their child. I decided I wanted to go into social work to help people like myself get connected with foster parents like mine. Then, when I learned how little social workers made, I changed my mind.

"You see, my parents—my foster parents, that is—lived on very little. I wanted to be able to provide for them, since they only had their Social Security for retirement. So I changed to accounting. I was always good with math and figured I would make more money in this profession.

"Now my foster parents live in a nice condo community near the bay, and they get to travel a lot. I work like a horse, but I love every minute of it because of the reward it brings."

Just a few moments before, Joe had wished someone else had come to lunch in his place. Now he wanted to reach across the table and hug this man he hardly knew. He continued to look directly into Bob's eyes, listening with all of his senses. He wanted Bob to keep talking. He complied.

"I don't plan to do this forever, though. As soon as I can, I want to start accepting foster kids into my home. Someday I hope to start an inner-city orphanage here in Seattle. You probably don't know this, Joe, but there are more kids being raised without parents in this country than ever before. And I want to do something, no matter how small, to help out."

Joe looked at Bob, knowing it was time to say something. But what? *How should I respond? Yesterday I would have ignored him. Now, after a simple lesson in listening, I feel like Bob is my friend.* He had accepted Bob simply by setting himself aside and inviting him to share his thoughts and feelings. Joe knew he could now build a relationship with this man. And what's more, he really wanted to.

"Bob, would you like to come to dinner at my house sometime next week? I would love to hear more. Perhaps there would even be a way I could pitch in to help you fulfill your dream."

CHAPTER 16

"I CAN'T believe it. I just can't believe it!" Joe vented his words with tight fists and through clenched teeth.

He had stopped at Mac's after work, not so much for coffee, but because he had to talk with someone. And there was no one he now trusted more than the coffee shop owner. When Joe walked into the shop, Mac could tell there was a storm raging. He let Joe calm down for a moment before asking if there was something he wanted to talk about.

"I feel like I've just been mugged. I work my tail off for Stuart, and they reward me like this."

Mac poured Joe a cup of iced coffee, a springtime special he had just brewed. They sat at a table near the counter so Mac could keep an eye on things.

"What's the matter?"

"They might take the AguCo account from me, that's what."

"Why would they do that?" Mac was concerned. "Aren't you the one who brought it to your agency?"

"Of course. But now they're accusing me of misusing the client's money. Alex Redding—he's in our accounting department—took a report to Mr. Stuart saying I was cooking the books on the AguCo account and overspending in TV production and graphics. What he didn't tell Stuart is that I'm way under budget in Web site design and in other promotions. I'm right on the money when it comes to the bottom line. And that's what counts. But there's a meeting tomorrow with Mr. Stuart to decide if I get to keep the account—and my job."

Mac asked why Joe thought Alex Redding would be accusing him if it wasn't true. Joe could tell Mac really cared, and he noticed the calming effect it had on him. His next response was quieter.

"Redding has always resented me. We started at the agency at the same time—as a matter of fact, we applied for the same job. But I had more experience in both the creative aspect and media than he did. They hired me in my area and offered him a lesser position in accounting. He went to school to get his degree in finance, but he always wanted to be in the creative side of things. I think he still feels he could do a better job than I could. He never seems very happy. He does sloppy work—and that's when he's there. He takes long lunches and leaves early almost every day. I don't know why Mr. Stuart has put up with him as long as he has. I'll tell you this, Mac: The day he gets fired will be the happiest day of my life."

Mac sipped from his ever-present cup of water, then slowly responded. "Joe, can you see the chain you're wearing?"

"Chain?"

"The chain that's binding you to Alex Redding. The shackles of bitterness and resentment. You're bound to him as surely as if there were a physical chain clamped to your ankle. Joe, when you resent someone, you become their slave."

Mac's response wasn't what Joe had expected. *I thought Mac would sympathize with me, tell me how I was being mistreated, agree that Alex Redding was doing me wrong. Instead, he seems to be laying the blame at my feet.*

"Joe, if what you're telling me about Alex is as you say—and I don't have reason to doubt you—you still have some responsibility. Maybe he *is* resentful of you. But you're still responsible, not for his actions but for your reactions. The truth will come out, Joe. It always does. In the meantime you have to be careful how you respond. You may be unfairly accused of a wrong you didn't commit. You may lose this account. But those things are minor compared with losing your spiritual and emotional well-being."

Joe had never seen such a serious expression on Mac's face. He had a thousand responses, but none surfaced. Joe remained silent.

"Pick up that sack at your feet," said Mac, indicating a large bag filled with roasted coffee beans.

Joe reached down to lift the burlap sack. He struggled to get it to his knees, then let it drop again.

"That sack weighs more than a hundred pounds. Imagine carrying it with you everywhere you go for the rest of your life. Its weight will only increase; it will never get lighter. I guarantee you'll be looking for a way to get rid of the sack altogether."

Joe looked down at the burlap bag once again, then turned his eyes back to Mac.

"How do I do that, Mac? I mean, he's the one who wronged me. Shouldn't he bear the load?"

Mac got up and went behind the counter to a chrome pot that sat apart from the others. He pushed on the pump and poured from the pot's contents into a mug. He returned and handed the mug to Joe.

"Take a sip of this coffee."

"If you don't mind, I'd rather not have coffee or a relationship lesson just now."

"Joe, please. Just take a sip."

Joe brought the cup to his lips. Even before he tasted the coffee, his nose picked up the bitter aroma. In one small slurp, he tasted the sour, burnt flavor. He set it down on the table and pushed it away from him, his face casting his vote.

"I left the pot on the burner too long. I was distracted. That's Papua New Guinea coffee, one of the best coffees in the world. Now it's worthless to us. Bitterness can't be taken out of coffee; it can only be put in. And once it's in, it ruins the entire pot."

Mac had an unusually stern tone in his voice, "You must do something that most people find very difficult. So difficult, many choose instead to become slaves to hatred. Their lives are stained through with bitterness.

"You have a choice to make, Joe. A very important choice that will affect every relationship you have from now on. You must choose whether to hold on to your hatred of Alex Redding, whether to allow bitterness to take root in your soul and spread to every area of your life. Or you can choose to forgive him, to let him go, to be free from his control."

Joe stared at the ceramic mug on the table. He knew his mentor was right. He could feel that resentment coursing through his spirit. *I don't want this terrible feeling. But how can I help it? Alex wronged me.*

"But if I forgive him, won't that show weakness? Won't others try to push me around too? Don't I need to stand up for myself?"

Mac countered, "The truth is, by following the example of Jesus Christ and forgiving others, you show great strength. You show that you can't be manipulated or controlled by what others do or say. The willingness to forgive is essential to keeping relationships strong. If you let bitterness have its way. . . . Well, you remember that coffee you just tasted?"

Joe left with a plastic bottle of chocolate milk Mac kept on hand for parents who came in with their kids. It helped to counter the taste of burnt coffee in his mouth. He also knew what he had to do the next day at work to get the taste of bitterness and hatred out of his spirit.

LESSON 5

BY FORGIVING OTHERS, YOU SHOW GREAT STRENGTH. THE WILLINGNESS TO FORGIVE IS ESSENTIAL TO KEEPING RELATIONSHIPS STRONG.

CHAPTER 17

"IN conclusion, Mr. Stuart," Alex Redding lectured in their mid-morning meeting, "I hesitate bringing this information to you. You know how much I value Joe's contribution to the firm. But I feel this, ah . . . indiscretion on his part is too great to let pass. I must bring it to your attention for the good of our client and our company."

Redding sat down as if he had just given a final statement to the jury. Joe was seated in a second chair in front of Stuart's desk. During Redding's remarks, Stuart had been looking through a stack of spreadsheets and memos in a tan legal-size folder. Now that Redding was finished, he looked up from the paperwork and directed himself to Joe.

"Do you have anything else to say?"

Joe had already explained his use of the AguCo money in constructing their campaign. He had done so without—or at least he thought without—pointing a finger of blame back at Alex Redding. He had simply shown that, yes, they had gone over budget on a couple of items, but they were under budget in other areas. When it was all tallied, they would still be within the ten-percent variance allowed in the contract.

He looked at Redding and then back to Mr. Stuart. "No, sir, not right now."

Stuart nodded, took one more look at the folder, and then closed it before looking straight at Redding.

"Alex, I have had my eye on you for some time. You may not know that, but very little gets by me in an agency as small as ours. You have never shown a passion for what we do here. But, be that as it may, I've kept you on because you have done competent, but not stellar, work in accounting."

Redding nervously tugged at the knot of his tie and looked down at the table. It was evident that he didn't like the way the conversation was going.

"But this accusation against Joe and his team is totally uncalled for. Not only have you slandered a good man, you have taken time away from the work you should have been doing to prepare this bogus report. Even a cursory glance at these numbers would tell you that nothing sinister is going on with this campaign.

"Joe is perfectly within his budget. I even took the time to call Bob Service, AguCo's contact in their accounting department, to ask if he is pleased with Joe's work. He told me that he has never had a better flow of information from a vendor. He said as far as he is concerned, Stuart Creative will have AguCo's account as long as Joe is with us.

"Alex, you've left me no option but to terminate your employment with us, effective immediately. I've already informed HR to make out your last check. You can pick it up on your way out."

Redding looked up at Mr. Stuart and started to say something, but he changed his mind. Instead, he slowly stood and turned toward the door.

"Mr. Stuart, may I say something?" Joe's voice stopped Redding, who turned and looked at the man he supposed should have been extremely satisfied with what had just happened.

"Mr. Stuart, I know that Alex did something wrong here. But I want to say something to him in front of you." Joe stood and faced Redding.

"Alex, I forgive you. I know you did this to undermine me, and I'm not really sure why. But that doesn't matter. I don't want you to leave feeling that I hate you, because I don't. I mean, I did yesterday, but not now. I don't want to become bitter." He held out his hand to Redding, who looked at it for a long time before he received it with his own.

"Mr. Stuart," Joe continued, "may I ask one more thing?" Stuart nodded.

"Sir, I know you have your reasons for letting Alex go, but I also know that this is going to be really hard on his family. His wife just had a baby, and there were some complications. I think surgery is planned." He looked at Redding, who nodded in affirmation.

"And with the job market being what it is, well, it may be tough for Alex to find something right now. Could you, well, reconsider?"

Stuart glanced at Redding, then back to Joe. He asked them both to sit down.

"Gentlemen, I will tell you I have never heard such a request. Joe, this man accused you of something that could have meant your dismissal. Fortunately, it had no merit. Now you're forgiving this man—and you want me to as well?"

Stuart shook his head, then smiled, then laughed. Long and hard and loud.

"Joe, you may have missed your calling. I know you're a great creative director, but do you ever think you should have been a minister instead?"

Outside in the hallway, following Stuart's admonition to work hard at what he was given to do and not to meddle where he shouldn't, Alex Redding turned to his new friend. "Joe, I don't know what to say. How did you know all that about my family?"

"I asked around this morning, Alex. I talked to a few people who told me about the hard time you and Sally are going through. I figured maybe the pressures you have at home are affecting what you're doing here."

"But why would you care? Especially after how I just treated you?"

"Alex, let's just say I don't want to be like a cup of burnt coffee." Knowing his statement wouldn't make any sense to the accountant, Joe suggested they get together for lunch later in the week, his treat. As they parted, the tears were trailing down Alex Redding's cheeks.

CHAPTER 18

THERE are rains, and then there are times when it seems the very air has turned to water. This Thursday morning was just like that. Joe knew it was hopeless to wait for a letup and was totally soaked after a short run from his car into the coffee shop. He went straight to the counter, reached over, and grabbed a towel. Standing by the fire, he wiped the water off his face and hair.

He heard raucous laughter. He whipped around to face the table behind him. Three men sat together—the same men at the same table that Joe had noticed every morning he visited Mac's Place. At first Joe thought they were directing their laughter at his wet condition. He was just about to confront the rude men when he realized that wasn't the case. Now he doubted that they even knew he was there, which upset him just as much as if he were the target of the joke.

"Excuse me," he said as he approached the men. "Have you seen Mac?"

The men pulled themselves together enough to respond.

"He had to leave for a while," said the lone member of the group who was wearing a suit and tie.

The other two were dressed more casually. "We're watching the store this morning—can I get you something?"

"No, thanks," Joe answered. "I was supposed to meet Mac here for . . ." He didn't know how to say, "a lesson on relationship building," so he let the sentence hang.

"Why not join us this morning?" asked another of the threesome. He wore khaki pants, a Seahawks sweatshirt, and running shoes. "Here, let me get you a chair. My name's Mick. This is Keith, and this is Charlie," introducing the man in the suit. Joe shook hands all around and introduced himself to the group. He saw that they each had in front of them the black leather books he had often wondered about. Upon closer inspection he discovered that these books were actually Bibles.

"I hope I'm not interrupting something," Joe said, taking a seat.

"Not at all," Mick replied. "We were just having our morning laugh. Charlie told us a funny story. Tell it again, Chuck. I think it's going to take several more times before I have it down enough to steal it."

Charlie didn't need any more prompting. He launched into a story that required a funny face, hand motions, and waving of the arms. There was only one other couple in the coffee shop; they stopped to listen and laughed out loud as Charlie delivered the punch line.

"How 'bout that, Joe?" Keith's voice was a high-pitched squeal, maybe because he was trying to talk while he laughed.

"That's a good one," Joe answered, swiping at tears of laughter. "As a matter of fact, I haven't really had that much to laugh about lately. Too busy, I guess."

The trio looked at one another and smiled. Mick took the lead.

"Joe, if you're not laughing very often, you're not taking good care of yourself. You know the saying 'Laughter is the best medicine'? Well, we've been studying about laughter this morning. Did you know it's in the Bible?"

At the mention of the Bible, Joe hesitated. He hadn't opened a Bible since his parents stopped making him go to Sunday school when he was in fifth grade.

"I'm not much of a Bible scholar," Joe mumbled.

The three men smiled. Keith said, "Neither are we. That's why we're here—to help each other with what we don't understand."

"I've noticed you guys here a lot," said Joe.

"We've been meeting here for, what, ten months now?" Mick asked his friends, who nodded in reply. "We get together every morning to encourage one another, then we call or e-mail throughout the day as needed. You see, Joe, we're all very needy people. The three of us especially."

Joe looked at the men. They were about his age, perhaps a little older. They looked to be in good health.

"For example," Keith answered Joe's unasked question, "my company is in the midst of corporate right-sizing. There's a good chance I'll be let go in the next week or so. I was pretty uptight about it yesterday until I got an e-mail from Mick. You know, with one of those top-ten lists that circulate throughout the Internet. It was just what I needed: a good old belly laugh to help me take my mind off my problems."

Charlie slid his Bible toward Joe. "See right here? In Proverbs it says, 'A cheerful heart is good medicine.' In one sense, we're each other's heart doctors." Keith responded to this description with another out-loud laugh.

"Yeah, and without submitting a bill to our health-care providers," Mick joined in.

"There are days I could use that kind of medicine," confessed Joe. "My job doesn't seem to be in jeopardy, but there's a lot of stress right now. I'm trying to think of a way to get my team to work harder to meet our deadlines, but they're already working fifty to sixty hours a week."

Mick, Charlie, and Keith looked at one another with a smile. Charlie said, "Why not make them laugh? I'll bet they could get that work done in fewer hours if they had some 'good medicine' running through their veins. Give it a try."

"Mac taught us about laughter some time ago. He said that people who love to laugh, who don't take themselves too seriously, are people others will want to work for—or be around."

"What's your e-mail address, Joe? I want to keep in touch with you." Mick and Charlie echoed Keith's request. Joe shared his work and home e-mail addresses and got his new friends' addresses in return.

"Thanks, guys. You've made me wealthier."

"How's that?" asked Charlie.

"Oh, just something between Mac and me." *It's strange that Mac isn't here.* He was about to ask if anyone knew why when Charlie spoke up.

LESSON 6

PEOPLE WHO LOVE TO LAUGH, WHO DON'T TAKE THEMSELVES TOO SERIOUSLY, ARE PEOPLE OTHERS WILL WANT TO BE AROUND.

"Sure glad to meet you, Joe. I've seen you in here a lot lately and have wanted to introduce myself. You're welcome to join us anytime."

"I just might take you up on that. One more thing . . ."

"Sure, Joe."

"Could you tell me that story one more time so I'm sure I've got it?"

CHAPTER 19

JOE had called a ten o'clock meeting of his team. But well before that he knew there was going to be trouble. Amanda had tried to storyboard three more television commercials, but the AguCo marketing liaison didn't like any of them. Mark was having problems with a network buy. A program he had said was instrumental in reaching their target audience was being canceled at the end of the season. Meanwhile, D'Juan had just broken up with his girlfriend. And Maria Alicia was losing the morning sickness war.

At 9:40, Joe went across the street to a doughnut shop and loaded a box with a dozen of their most-requested. He also made a stop at a convenience store to buy a gallon of orange juice and a box of crackers for Maria Alicia. Armed with the requisite for a successful corporate meeting—food—Joe went to the conference room and wrote on the whiteboard in big, bold letters, "WE KNOW HOW TO TELL THE STORY."

The other members of the team strolled in a few minutes before the top of the hour. Leslie came in first, bypassed the doughnuts, and went straight to Joe with a problem she was having with Amanda regarding graphics for a coupon insert. Joe asked her to save her question for later and invited her to have a doughnut. By that time Mark and D'Juan had arrived; they needed no encouragement to reach for the goodies. Amanda followed the men and then stopped to advise Joe, "Maria Alicia will be here in a minute. She's in the bathroom throwing up."

Amanda's comment was enough to make Joe pass on the doughnut he had been eyeing for himself. Instead, he took the box of saltines and placed it where the expectant mother would be sitting, then he drank a cup of orange juice.

"What's that on the board, Joe?" Leslie inquired. "What story?"

"I'm glad you asked, Leslie. I'm going to tell you in a few moments."

Just then, Maria Alicia arrived, looking the same shade of green as her new maternity blouse. She thanked her boss for the saltines.

Joe got their attention and began his version of the tale he had heard at Mac's Place:

"Many years ago in a mountainous region of Europe, there was a little-known monastery. The monastery owned all the land at the top of a mountain and down the grassy slope to the valley at the bottom. In the valley was a village with common people who lived there courtesy of the monastery.

"The monastery began to grow. And soon the monks were so crowded, two brothers had to share a room—and the same wash basin. The decision was made to expand the monastery, but the only site was in the valley where the villagers lived."

D'Juan asked loudly, through a mouthful of doughnut, "What are you talking about? What does this have to do with AguCo?"

Joe ignored D'Juan and continued on with the story.

"A representative from the monastery called on the villagers to tell them they would have to move. They were shocked. 'We have always lived here,' they said. 'You can't kick us out!'

"'Actually, we can,' replied the stern monk. 'We own this land.'

"The villagers sighed in unison.

"'But, in the spirit of fairness,' the monk continued, 'we'll give you a chance to keep your land. Tomorrow we will have a great contest. Our Father Prior will descend from the mountain and debate one of you villagers. He'll give you the rules. If he wins—which no doubt he will—you must leave. But if by some chance you win, you may stay.'

"The villagers had no choice.

"As the sun rose, a solitary monk made his way down the mountain. In the square, all the villagers had gathered for the debate.

"They selected a young man to do the debating. His name was Fred."

Amanda started to giggle. Joe remembered that she had once dated a man named Fred and figured she found him—or just the name—funny.

"Fred and the Father Prior met in the middle of the square, where a simple wooden table and two wooden chairs had been placed. The Father Prior bowed toward the crowd, bowed toward Fred, and then spoke.

"'Today's contest will decide who will control this valley. There will be a three-point debate regarding the sovereignty of the Almighty. But neither debater may use any words.' The Father Prior then took his seat.

"Fred also sat down at the table, opposite the monk. He had two problems. First, he didn't know how he would get three points across without using words, and second, he had no earthly idea what *sovereignty* meant.

"The Father Prior began by extending his index finger high into the air—reaching so high that the long underwear under his robe showed slightly—sending a subdued giggle through the collective ladies in the square.

"Fred responded to the monk's challenge. He shook his head and boldly held three fingers in the air.

"The Father Prior's eyes suddenly enlarged.

"Quickly, the monk spread his arms as wide as they would go, almost bursting open his robe.

"Fred pondered the move, shook his head again, and pointed to the ground.

"Giant beads of sweat popped out on the monk's uncovered head, and he began to mop them with a hand that trembled so that he was barely able to find his forehead.

"Exasperated, the Father Prior slowly reached into his robe and pulled out a warm loaf of bread and a chilled bottle of wine, placing them both on the table.

"Now the sweat was on Fred's forehead. Fred leaned over and reached into a beat-up leather satchel, pulled out an apple, took a bite, then set it on the table next to the warm bread and the chilled wine.

"The monk immediately stood, threw up his hands, and screamed, 'HE WINS! THE SIMPLE VILLAGER HAS WON THE DEBATE!' The crowd cheered as the Father declared, 'You may stay in the village.'"

Leslie and Mark said at the same time, "I don't get it."

Joe carried on. "The monk trudged slowly back up the hill to the monastery, where the brothers met him, wanting a play-by-play.

"'Brothers,' he began sadly, 'I have failed. The villagers have won.'

"'No, Father!' they cried. 'How can it be?' Fiddling with the tassel on his robe, the Father Prior tried to explain how he lost the debate without using a single word.

"'I began by declaring there is but one Almighty. But the villager responded by showing that He is *three* unique beings in one.'

"The brothers looked at one another in astonishment.

"'Next, I declared that the Almighty has made all that there is and is far above us. The simple villager responded by pointing to the earth and declaring that the Almighty also came down to live as one of us.'

"The brothers began to fidget.

"'Finally, I took out the bread and wine to symbolize the sacrifice of the Almighty. But the villager took out an apple to show that without Adam's sin there would have been no need for the sacrifice.'

"The brothers fell to their knees and began to moan, holding their half-shaved heads in their hands. There was much crying and wailing into the night."

Here, Joe paused for effect. He had his team's complete attention. "Meanwhile, back in the village Fred was telling another version to the amazed crowd, who wondered how he had pulled off a win.

"'I don't rightly know,' Fred shouted above the noise. 'That monk fella started by telling me we only had *one* day to clear out, but I told him we needed at least *three* to pack up all the pigs and the kids.

"'Then he spread his arms out, saying he owned all this here land. So I pointed down to let him know it would take more than one guy in a dress to move me and the missus off this piece of ground.'

"The crowd was thrilled at Fred's boldness. 'What happened next?'

"'Well, then he stopped for lunch.'

"'Lunch?' Fred's mother chimed in.

"'Yep!' Fred said. 'Good thing I brought that apple.'"

At first, Joe's team just looked at one another. Joe wasn't usually a storyteller. Amanda looked down at the table and started to giggle. It wasn't long before the giggles began to spread like a bad cold. In only a few moments, the giggles were sent to the dugout, and sidesplitting, tears-on-your-face, it's-not-that-funny-but-I-can't-stop laughter took to the field. The sight was hilarious.

When they had finally quieted down, Joe spoke up.

"I tell that story for two reasons. First, because it's a pretty good story, and I thought we could all use a laugh. But, second, because I wanted to remind us all—myself included—that we know how to tell stories. Amanda, you're the best I know at coming up with effective TV spots. You won't let us down. Mark, you'll find an even better program to place the spots on. I believe we're the best ad team AguCo could ever have. So, let's just relax, finish these doughnuts, pull out our laptops, and get back to the drawing board."

Joe set another touch-base meeting for 4:30 that afternoon. When they regrouped, Amanda showed the team her storyboards for three television spots she and D'Juan had worked on. When she was finished, the team burst into applause. Amanda blushed and said, "C'mon, guys, they're not that good."

Mark reported he had leads on avails for two other programs and might even come in under budget. Again there was applause.

"I told you we're a great team," Joe bragged. "Now get out of here! Go enjoy the rest of the evening."

No one argued. As they excitedly gathered their notebooks and other belongings to make a fast exit, Mark stopped Joe and said, "Can you tell us that story one more time? I want to make sure I have it right."

On his way home, Joe stopped by Mac's Place to see if he was there and to report on his efforts that day. Charlie was behind the counter, filling a chrome pot with Kenya AA.

"Hi, Charlie. Have you seen Mac?"

Charlie quickly placed the pot on the counter and responded in a soft, sad voice.

"Joe, Mac is in the hospital. The doctors have discovered an aggressive cancer. He's been keeping it from us. But now I'm afraid he's in really bad shape."

CHAPTER 20

THERE *is no such thing as a warm hospital,* Joe thought. *The beds, the chairs, the curtains, even the floor, say, "This isn't really home."* He made the turn down the hallway to Room 1013, knowing he wasn't really prepared for what he was about to see.

Marcy had told him to expect Mac to be heavily sedated. She said having a brain tumor can be extremely painful, but it mercifully claims its victims quickly. Marcy said Mac would be made comfortable but probably wouldn't be able to go home again. Hospice would be available to him in the hospital.

Surprisingly, Mac was sitting up in bed and was fairly alert. He looked peaceful, or as peaceful as one can look with tubes in his arms and up his nose. He was gazing out the window but turned his head when he heard Joe walk in.

"Hey, friend. Thanks for coming." His voice was barely above a whisper.

"I had to, Mac. I haven't had a decent cup of coffee in days."

Mac laughed weakly. "Neither have I. It tastes like they work overtime to make this stuff taste as bad as possible. So, I hear you met the Three Stooges—Mick, Charlie, and Keith?"

"Yeah, great guys." From the way Mac said their names, Joe could tell that they were special to him. "Have they been up to visit?"

"All three. This morning. I wasn't very alert. I don't even remember how long they stayed. But I do remember Charlie reading from the Psalms. I do remember that. I don't have a lot of time left."

Joe tried to interrupt.

"No, don't try to lie to me. The doctors have been honest enough. And you know nurses don't lie! By the way, Joe, your wife stopped in to see me during her lunch break. She's a keeper. . . .

"I'm so thankful we got to know each other. I knew the first time we met that you have what it takes to gain true wealth." Mac pointed weakly toward the bedside table.

"See that envelope? There's a note in there for you. It has to do with the coffee shop. But don't open it just yet. I have something I want to talk with you about. Your final lesson."

Mac's voice was so weak, his student had a hard time making out what he was saying.

"Let's talk another time. I think you need some rest."

Mac reached over and gripped Joe's hand as it rested on the bed railing. "Joe, there may not be another time."

He continued, almost in a whisper, "And what I have to tell you is the most important of all. You've learned well. But if you don't get this last one, nothing else will really matter. You'll never become as rich as you want to be."

Joe pulled his chair as close to the bed as he could. "What's the last one, Mac? What is it?"

His best friend closed his eyes, which somehow gave his voice a small boost. It was almost as if he transferred the energy it took to keep his eyes open to his lungs.

"My darling wife, Maggie, and I had one son. His name was Michael." Joe picked up on the use of the past tense.

"Maggie died giving birth. She had been very sick throughout the pregnancy, and the doctors said she used her last bit of energy to bring Michael into the world. At first I was lost as a single parent. I struggled to take care of a baby and build a business at the same time. Looking back, I'm sure I didn't spend enough time building a relationship with my son. But, still, he turned out to be a good boy."

"I'm sure you did all you could," Joe encouraged.

"Michael did well in school and was something of a star athlete. He had a few football offers from some colleges but decided to go to the University of Idaho to become a forest-fire fighter. And he did. He was so happy when he graduated, but he was even more excited when he called me after his first fire. He delighted in trying to save the forests from being destroyed.

"Then one day I got the call. Michael and three others were killed in one of the worst fires Idaho has ever seen. He was given a hero's funeral. When I got home, I went over his whole life in my mind.

"I had told him that he was a good boy, that he was a good student, and a good football player. When he was older, I told him how proud I was of him for pursuing his dreams and that I was proud he was a firefighter.

"But I can never remember a single time I told him I loved him. Not once."

Joe helped Mac take a sip of water, bending the straw to his dried, cracked lips. Mac managed to draw a few drops from the glass, then settled back on his pillow.

"I never said 'I love you' to my own son. The thought of that causes me more pain than all the cancer in the world. Joe, your last lesson—from me, anyway—is this: Learn to say 'I love you.' Say it often. Say it with your mouth, your eyes, your hands, your feet. There are no more powerful words in our language."

These last words were no more than a raspy breath. Mac's head gently turned to one side; he was asleep. Joe remained with his friend for another half-hour, holding his hand, weeping for the man he had just begun to know, who was now being taken from him. The charge nurse came by and gently told him it would be best if Mac would sleep.

Without looking back toward the bed, Joe picked up the envelope on the table and slipped it in his jacket pocket as he quietly made his way out of the room. By now, the parking lot was as empty as the feeling in his heart.

As he drove, he found himself drawn to Mac's Place. It was after midnight; the store was dark. The "Closed" sign hung in the door.

Somehow the sight of this sign overcame Joe. Waves of tears flowed from deep inside. A saying passed through his mind: "Weeping may stay for the night, but rejoicing comes in the morning." *Where have I heard that? Perhaps in church when I went with my parents?*

LESSON 7

LEARN TO SAY I LOVE YOU. SAY IT OFTEN. SAY IT WITH YOUR MOUTH, YOUR EYES, YOUR HANDS, YOUR FEET. THERE ARE NO MORE POWERFUL WORDS IN OUR LANGUAGE.

Joe was sure he had enough tears to last through the night. But when morning came, would there be any rejoicing?

CHAPTER 21

JOE had not missed a day of work in more than a year, but he knew he would be worthless there today, so he called in to request a personal day. Marcy had the day off. She said she would go to the hospital with him to visit Mac, but that they should wait until after ten o'clock to give the doctors and nurses time to do their evaluations and administer medications.

"Marcy," Joe said as he took his wife by the hand and led her to the couch. "Sit down for a moment, please. I want to talk with you."

Marcy sat down and, keeping her hand in Joe's, looked for a moment directly into his eyes, then past them ever so slightly. Joe stared directly into his wife's beautiful, dark green eyes.

"I really don't know what to do or what to say right now. Mac has become a good friend in such a short time. But, more than that, he has taught me more than I could have ever imagined.

"Marcy, I've learned a lot from him these past few weeks. I've learned some fun stuff about coffee, but that was just a handy object for the real lessons he taught me. When I first went to his shop, he handed me a coupon for a free cup of coffee. On the back there was a message: 'Are you as rich as you want to be? Ask Mac.' So I asked him. He told me that true riches have nothing to do with money. He said the real measure of a man's wealth lies in the relationships he has with himself and with others. He revealed seven life lessons to me. May I share them with you?"

Marcy nodded her head.

"First, before you can be friends with others, you have to be friends with yourself."

He told his wife about his trip to the mountain and his memories of his dad's words to him. He said he left many of his hurts and pains on the mountain that night and left with the feeling that he could be a good friend to others.

"Next, Mac taught me that in order to have friends, one has to be a friend. That's how Al and I got to be friends. I made the first move, and now look—we get together for running or AA meetings almost every day.

"For my third lesson, Mac showed me how easy and how much fun it is to speak encouraging words to others. I made a game of it one day and had one of the best days at work ever. It felt so good sharing positive comments that I kept trying to find someone else to encourage. I think it became contagious because I've noticed how several other people in my office now speak more kindly to each other."

Joe paused while he tried to think of the next lesson in spite of the overwhelming emotions he was feeling.

"Oh yes, the taste test Mac called 'cupping.'

"The fourth lesson Mac taught me was about listening. I mean really listening—listening in a careful way. I tried that with Bob Service at lunch the next day, and then you got to meet him at dinner last week. You see what kind of person he is and how you and I are becoming his friends. Who knows how this will turn out—I mean, with his dream of an orphanage and all.

"The next lesson—the fifth life lesson—was the hardest to apply. Remember when I came home steaming because of what Alex Redding had done?" Marcy said she remembered all too well.

"Well," Joe continued, "I had actually let out most of my steam at Mac's Place before I came home. He taught me that if I held on to my anger, if I let it become hatred and bitterness, I would be a slave to Alex. Mac showed me that I needed to forgive Alex, to let go of my hatred. And somehow, the next day in Mr. Stuart's office, I was able to do it. I think I shocked Mr. Stuart and Alex. And, to tell the truth, I shocked *me!* But it felt as if I had just laid down, well, a hundred-pound sack of coffee beans.

"The next lesson came yesterday from three guys at Mac's Place—Mick, Keith, and Charlie. They're the ones who gave me the story about the monk and the villagers." Marcy rolled her eyes just as she had the first time when Joe had called home from work and told it to her. "The lesson I learned from that story was to not take myself or others too seriously. To laugh a lot. I learned that laughing is actually very good medicine."

Joe stopped and looked away. When he turned back to Marcy, his cheeks were wet with tears.

"And now, just as I'm beginning to feel like I understand what Mac was talking about when he referred to 'true wealth,' just when I think I'm starting to learn these lessons, he's being taken away from me. I don't understand. I just don't understand!"

Marcy stroked her husband's shoulder with her free hand. "Joe, you said there were seven lessons."

Joe looked deep into Marcy's eyes. "Marcy, last night Mac told me that the seventh lesson is the most important. I think it's going to be hardest to apply. But I'm going to try.

"Marcy, I love you. I know I haven't been the best husband in the world, but I want to be. You deserve the best. And I want to start by saying this more often: I love you."

He let the words linger in the quiet air for a moment before he spoke again.

"You've had some tough times, Marcy. I know your home life wasn't real good. But I want you to know how much I love you. And if you'll let me, I'll say those words to you every day for the rest of my life. I really do love you."

Marcy took her hand from Joe's and looked down at the floor. When she spoke, her voice was soft, like a child's.

"Why do you love me? I'm nothing special. I'm sure there are lots of better wives out there."

It was a moment of discovery. Joe understood now—if not fully, at least in part—why all these years his wife would not look him in the eye, why she shied away from intimacy. He had always thought maybe he wasn't doing something right or wasn't saying things in the right way. Now he knew it had nothing to do with him. Marcy often didn't act like she was receiving his love because she didn't love herself. Marcy needed to start with lesson one—she needed to learn to like herself.

"Marcy, I want to say something to you, and I want you to hear me. I love you. I think you're wonderful. As a matter of fact, you're my best friend." At these last words, Marcy looked up.

"You are my best friend. I love you, Marcy, and I love being with you."

Now Marcy was the one crying. She began with a few tears that quickly escalated to sobs. Joe let her cry, figuring this was the best way for his beloved wife to wash away years of guilt and self-doubt. After a while, sobbing in Joe's arms, she calmed down. Joe asked if she was all right. She nodded slowly, then did what she seldom did—and what Joe longed for.

She looked into his eyes, holding his gaze for nearly a minute. Then she bent her head against his shoulder and whispered, "From the very first day . . . from the day we first met, I've loved you . . . and I always will."

Later, as they sat together on their covered porch, Joe talked with Marcy about the pleasantness he felt in Mac's Place. "One just feels at peace there," he said. "It would be a shame to see it closed. But since Mac had no partner and no heir, he didn't know what else to do."

"You do."

"What?"

Marcy explained, "I think you know exactly what to do."

Joe nodded and once again read the legal-looking letter that had been in the envelope next to Mac's hospital bed.

CHAPTER 22

EVERYONE who was acquainted with Mac knew he hated funerals. "Funerals are for the dead," he often said. "And since they're dead, what do they care?" So Mac's friends had the idea of an old-fashioned wake. One week after Mac's passing, the coffee shop was opened once again to an overflow crowd.

"I've never seen it this crowded," Mick shouted into Joe's ear. "How did all these people know about this?"

"Oh, I may have mentioned it here and there," Joe said with a laugh. "I thought they would want to pay their respects to Mac."

"But a lot of them have never met Mac."

"That's true," Joe replied. "But they know the difference Mac made in my life in such a short time. I guess that's enough for them."

Al Simpkins came up to the counter for a refill from the Mac's Blend pot. "This is great, Joe. This is a real nice thing you and your friends are doing."

"Thanks, Al. I'm glad you could make it. Do you like the coffee?"

"I should say—best I've ever had! I think you'll be seeing me in here more often."

"I hope so, Al, because this is where I'll be spending much of my time."

"Has the paperwork been approved yet?"

"Not yet," Joe answered. "But the judge gave me temporary power of attorney over Mac's estate to keep things going until it's finalized. And by the way, I need an assistant manager. Would you consider the job?"

"You bet I would!" Al exclaimed.

"Then you're hired," Joe said.

Joe looked up to see Amanda, D'Juan, Leslie, and Mark enter the shop, followed by Mr. Stuart.

"Excuse me a minute, Al, will you?"

Joe went around the counter to the door and greeted his former team from Stuart Creative. They took in the warmth of the cozy coffeehouse; Leslie edged her way toward the fireplace.

"So, this is what you're leaving us for?" Mr. Stuart's voice had a gruff edge, but the smile on his face betrayed him.

"Yes, sir," Joe said. "Someone has to carry on the legacy. The day before Mac died, he showed me a copy of his new will. He left me his estate, which consisted of this shop and a sizable sum to keep it running. He didn't exactly ask me to quit my job and come here full time, but I know he'd be pleased."

"Well, we're not pleased that you're leaving us just as we're set to roll out the AguCo campaign," Mark spoke up. "That just means more work for each of us."

"Now, Mark, I told you I'd be available to consult with you throughout the life of the campaign. And I hope it's a long life indeed."

"Joe is on retainer as a consultant for two years, and I'm sure we'll extend that as necessary." Mr. Stuart had been very generous to Joe, allowing him to keep the promised bonus and guaranteeing him enough as a consultant so he wouldn't have to worry about earning an income from selling coffee, at least for a couple of years.

"You see," he told Joe privately in his office when Joe told him of his desire to quit, "I had a Mac who invested in my life. The agency where I began was owned by a man named Jim Mason. He taught me about life and the value of friends, using advertising as a background for our lessons. When it was time for me to open my own agency, Mr. Mason gave me several of his best clients. So I understand why you feel you have to do this, Joe. I may not like it, but I think I understand."

Joe got a coffee for each of his colleagues—and tea for Amanda—then excused himself. He went back to the counter and banged a spoon on one of the pots to get everyone's attention.

"Thanks for coming to Mac's wake. I know he would appreciate it. There are only a couple of things I want to say."

"Well, keep it short," Mick shouted. "Charlie is in the middle of another one of his stories."

There was laughter all around. Joe looked up to see a customer—one he had never seen before—slip in the front door.

"I will, Mick, I will. Actually, that was the first thing I was going to mention: No long faces or sad words here tonight. Mac never felt sorry for himself, even up to the last minute. I'm sure he would be pretty upset with us if we made this a gloomy affair.

"Second, I've heard several people ask if I'll be changing the name of this joint to Joe's Place. The answer is an emphatic NO! As long as I have anything to do with it, this is and always will be Mac's Place."

"Here, here!" Keith and Charlie lifted their coffee mugs in a mock toast.

"And finally, I want to take this occasion to announce a new program we're introducing." Joe reached behind the counter and lifted up a large ceramic coffee mug. "This is our bottomless cup," he said proudly.

"Hard to hold coffee in a bottomless cup, isn't it?" Charlie was on a roll tonight.

"You can clean up all the spills, Charlie." Joe's reply got a good laugh. "Here's how this works. For $150, you get one of these fancy mugs—and all the coffee you want for a year. And here's the great part: Half of your money will go toward an orphanage we hope to see opened as soon as possible." There was a round of applause at the mention. "You can talk to my wife, Marcy—whom I love dearly—about the plans for that. We're working with Bob Service," Joe nodded to the small, balding, grinning man seated at one of the tables, "to bring this dream to life."

Joe finished his speech and worked his way back around the counter. People turned back to their discussions or to finish their stories about Mac. The new customer wormed his way through the crowd to the counter.

"Good evening," Joe said. "Welcome to Mac's Place. What can I get for you?"

"Well," the man said, "I normally don't drink coffee, but somehow it sounded good tonight. So I guess I'll just have a small cup to go." He looked to his left, then to his right. "Is it always this crowded?"

"This is a special occasion. The founder and owner of this shop passed away recently, and we have gathered as a tribute to him."

"Oh," the man said. "I didn't mean to intrude."

"Not a problem—you're very welcome to join us."

"Well, actually, a wake is probably just what I need."

"What do you mean?" Joe asked, with a slight tingle in his spine.

"I don't know, really. I mean, I moved here a month or so ago to take a job, and the job itself is great. But I really haven't met anyone other than those I work with, and they all have families. So I'm just kind of lonely, I guess."

Joe topped off the cup and put a plastic lid on it before handing it across the counter.

"You've come to the right place! By the way, my name's Joe. What's yours?"

"I'm Gary," said the man. "How much do I owe you?"

Joe smiled and said, "There's no charge for our first-timers. And, Gary, here's a coupon for you to use the next time you come in. I know it's kind of wrinkled, but I think you may find it will come in handy when you need it."

ABOUT THE AUTHOR

An international speaker, best-selling author and compassionate teacher, Stan has authored more than 100 books to date. Best sellers include *God Has Never Failed Me, but He's Sure Scared Me to Death a Few Times; The Buzzards Are Circling, but God's Not Finished with Me Yet; ReThink Your Life;* his popular Minute Motivators series; and his newest book, *TERRIFIC! Five Star Customer Service.* His books have sold more than three million copies worldwide.

Stan served for 40 years as a pastor. In addition to his writing, he was vice president of John Maxwell's Injoy Ministries, has spoken in 80 countries, and shared the platform with speakers that include Zig Ziglar, Jerry Lucas, Rick Warren, Bill Hybels, and Cy Young Award winner R. A. Dickey.

To contact the author visit www.stantoler.com.